PRAISE FOR BE THEIR WARRIOR

"With the strongest language at my command, I recommend *Be Their Warrior*. I've observed Pamela Hall's teaching thousands of times, and she applies with love and expertise the strategies shared in this book. This book is a tool kit of classroom moves, communication techniques, and self-help for instructors and trainers. It needs to be required reading for all administrators and teachers."

— DR. DAVID MARKEWITZ, PRINCIPAL

"Great vigor, courage and strength are evident throughout Pamela Hall's heart-inspired book about being a warrior for ALL students. Interwoven throughout are powerful and impactful stories that demonstrate how to create a responsive culture, how to effectively build relationships with all stakeholders, and how to be strong as a warrior starting with self. The heartwarming personal examples resonate so deeply with many of the same practices I found so effective in my own educational journey. All students deserve great opportunities to succeed and can do so when they have their own warrior fighting for them and believing in them. Learn how through this truly inspiring and uplifting book!"

— LIVIA CHAN, ELEMENTARY HEAD TEACHER,
AUTHOR, AND DIGITAL CONTENT COORDINATOR
FOR THE TEACH BETTER TEAM

"*Be Their Warrior* is a dynamic book filled with inspiration, motivation, and impact for every educator. Get ready to laugh, feel empowered, and connect to the heart of the author, as she shares her personal journey through education. Throughout her journey she learned how to be STRONG and provides detailed examples throughout the entire book on how you can remain true and strong to who you are as the educator you are within. This book will provide you with the "how" to go along with your inner why as a passionate educator. It's a must read for every educator, in any grade level, to read at any point during the school year!"

— LINDSAY TITUS, EDUCATOR AND MINDSET
COACH AND SPEAKER WITH DEFINE
YOUNIVERSITY

"You will never fully understand the depth of impact you had on a student's life! As educators, we must take the time to get to know our students. I always say we must do the 'heart-work' before doing the 'hard work.' For educators to be true agents of change, we must be comfortable disrupting the status quo and fostering authentic, equitable environments for all students to thrive. Each chapter unpacks a core principle related to culture, community, relationships, real educational vignettes, and practical, realistic takeaways. It helps you break down roadblocks and barriers that prohibit all students from being successful and allows educators to take the next steps toward being a warrior for students. *Be Their Warrior* is the perfect book and resource for every educator who is serious about fostering inclusive learning environments."

— DR. BASIL MARIN, HS ASSISTANT
PRINCIPAL/DEI CONSULTANT

"Students will often do nothing to help themselves if there is no one fighting for them. Hall brilliantly unleashes the 'warrior' concept for you with three core principles about culture, community, and how to be S.T.R.O.N.G.. With practical tips and reminders about the deep heart and soul of education and calling for all of us to be brave soldiers, alongside her, Hall arms us with not only a good read for the benefit of our students and schools everywhere, but brings to you a thoughtful, epic journey that will equip all of us to be 'warriors' for a lifetime."

— DR. RICK JETTER, CO-FOUNDER OF PUSHING
BOUNDARIES CONSULTING, LLC AND AUTHOR OF
9 BOOKS, INCLUDING THE HIGHLY ACCLAIMED
100 STOP SERIES

"An authentic story of creating a positive impact in the lives of our students, *Be Their Warrior* guides us through three principles and offers practical strategies to help all educators make the world a better place for our children. All students deserve to experience success in their lives, and Pamela Hall shows how we CAN make a difference."

— KAREN CASWELL EXPERIENCED EDUCATOR
AND LIFELONG LEARNER

"As soon as I started reading, *Be Their Warrior*, I was pulled into Pamela Hall's personal stories of children who struggled and eventually had their basic social, emotional, safety, and security needs met. It was clear in Pam's book that the foundation of any successful school is relationships focusing on what matters most-- kids. Every chapter includes heart-wrenching stories along with strategies, ideas, and reflection questions for teachers who want to empower kids to take risks in learning so they can learn effectively. This is a must-read for educators who want to be STRONG and be that warrior for the kids."

— BARBARA BRAY, CREATIVE LEARNING
STRATEGIST, PODCAST HOST, KEYNOTER, COACH,
AUTHOR OF *DEFINE YOUR WHY*

BE THEIR WARRIOR

Helping All Students Succeed Through Culture, Community, & Being STRONG

PAMELA HALL

PUBLISHING

ISBN: 978-1-953852-56-4

CONTENTS

For Mrs. Robinson, my parents, and all warriors who believed in me and shaped me.

&

To

All imperfect educators like me who strive to be a warrior for all kids. YOU make a difference!

INTRODUCTION

Her name was Mrs. Robinson. She loved to eat plain M & M's by the pound and drive us all around in her big white GMC to experience culture, history, camping, and life. We were scrawny, snot-nosed, 3rd graders she helped raise into our awkward pimpled teens. One time while driving us around Seattle, the old GMC made a thumping noise as we bounced around inside; she had run over a median strip and cursed, "Damn, damn, damn!" Followed by lamenting, "Oh, girls, I'm sorry, sorry, sorry." She was geographically lost, but she had a purpose: to show us life beyond a tiny rural town and expose us to opportunities. She was our Girl Scout leader. She was my champion, my warrior.

Mrs. Robinson planted the seed of greatness in me by building a relationship and demonstrating her unshakable belief in me. She taught me to set goals and stretch beyond what I thought was possible. She gave me lead roles in musical productions, which taught me to have confidence. Mrs. Robinson took me to prospective colleges when I didn't even think college was an option; no one from my family had ever gone to college, and my high school counselor told me my SAT scores were so low I'd never succeed. Despite the odds, I went to college. Even though I received an F during my first semester, I graduated with honors. Mrs. Robinson's belief in me shaped my life and influenced me to believe in myself and others.

She taught me to take advantage of opportunities, work hard, serve others, be a good citizen, sing, dance, and live every moment to the fullest. I'm forever grateful for her and all the *Mrs. Robinsons* in my life. Shouldn't everyone have a Mrs. Robinson in their life? Someone who believes in them and never ever gives up. Maybe you were fortunate enough to have a teacher or leader to bring out the best in you. But maybe you weren't. Regardless, *you* can be a warrior for your students. You can transform their lives. You, my friend, make a difference.

Being a warrior for *all* students needs to be as urgent as breathing. Building relationships with kids, having passion and energy, and going the extra mile sets you apart as a warrior. Loving and caring for students and desiring to make a difference comes naturally to most educators; it's why you do what you do. However, it takes establishing habits and intentional planning to utilize the limited time you have to focus on what matters most—kids. By following the principles in this book, you'll not only continue to love and believe in *all* your students, but you'll have some concrete ideas of how to champion their unique needs.

SETTING THE STAGE

Bay ran wildly through the door, dumping out all the bins of manipulatives that were neatly stored on shelves. Now, they were strewn across the room. It was open-house night. I ignored the wildness as I spoke encouragingly and lovingly to her mom. It's important to welcome all people kindly regardless of their child's behavior, right? Making a caring connection and first impression is paramount to future communication. When you establish the right relationships and connections, everything else follows. (Even modifying behavior.)

The first day of school arrived. Bay wet her pants countless times. She was six years old. Shouldn't she be potty trained by now? The class watched as I nonchalantly cleaned up and provided clean clothes. The way you respond transfers to how the class will treat your precious student. Respond with love and kindness. Always. For weeks, this went on: puddles in chairs or on the floor, clean up, provide clean clothes, encourage, and repeat. After expressing my concern to a colleague, she suggested using a timer so that after every hour, Bay would know to go to the bathroom before an accident occurred. Voila! It worked. We were able to reduce the incidents to one time a day. Consult with colleagues to find solutions to meet *all* students' needs. Our colleagues are a wealth of knowledge. They often help us see answers we can't see because we're too close to the situation.

One day, I learned Bay lived in a shed with no running water. Also, she came to school hungry, with her shoes pinching her toes and her clothes soiled, smelling like pungent, smoky urine. At the same time, when I saw all my students' data flash on a screen in front of my colleagues, I felt pressure to bring her up to grade-level in reading. Academically, she was low, low, low. My reading coach inquired about my action plan for helping Bay read on grade-level. I was thinking: *I just want her to go one day without wetting her pants and to engage in learning instead of crawling on the floor licking her hands like paws and meowing!*

After that meeting, I slipped into a secluded room and sobbed. The burden of helping students achieve grade-level expectations while overcoming basic needs obstacles pierced my heart and soul. What are we to do in these situations? What are we to do to help *all* students learn and hold it together emotionally and physically?

Unless we do something differently, students like Bay don't have much of a future. "Simple truth: Before expecting students to reach their potential, teachers need to meet students at their current levels" (Kline, n.d.). In today's society, the average class's makeup consists of students from diverse situations: affluent, poverty-stricken, broken family ties, incarceration of a family member, substance abuse, special needs, struggling with mental health, hungry, tired, and the list goes on. (Insert *your* class situations.) To top it off, current research states, "more than half of all U.S. children have experienced some kind of trauma in the form of abuse, neglect, violence, or challenging household circumstances—and 35% of children have experienced more than one type of traumatic event" (Minero, 2017).

Stating the obvious: About six out of 10 students in our class, no matter the age, have experienced an Adverse Childhood Experience(ACE). These statements aren't intended to be judgmental. I know that families send us the best they've got. For me, I sometimes forget the reality we face. We have to look reality square in the face to create an action plan.

When you look at developmental psychology, what are the ramifications we face day to day? Even though many are talking about "Maslow before Bloom," we need to consider the steps to reach every single smiling face—our students—every day.

"As Maslow proposed in his hierarchy of human needs, basic needs must be met before students can turn their attention to learning. After securing food, water, shelter, and safety from harm, people seek as their next most important needs affection, belonging, and esteem" (Powell & Kusuma-Powell, 2011). In the process of coming to know students, a caring and interested teacher develops rapport and trust. Trust and acceptance create a psychologically safe atmosphere in the classroom and school. Consequently, meeting *all* students' basic, social, emotional, safety, and security needs allows them to feel like taking risks in learning and being able to learn effectively, ultimately leading to high student engagement and achievement.

Image by Pamela Hall. Source: Root. (2017, September 20). Home. 2020 Printable calendar posters images wallpapers free. https://printablegraphics.in/maslow-hierarchy-needs-diagram/.

How can we be their warrior if we don't know where our students are coming from or their challenges when trying to learn? That's the heart of this book. Being a warrior is doing whatever it takes for *all* students to succeed. The strategies are designed to recognize and meet students' social, emotional, and academic needs daily. (Some strategies may be new to you, and some may validate what you do. Because, after all, best practices are best practices.)

By the end of the year, Bay quit wetting her pants. She was only a fraction away from grade-level expectations as opposed to several levels. She still crawled on the floor on occasion, but she became a contributing member of our class. One day while she was working on a project, she had glue dripping on the floor, scraps of paper everywhere, and her supply box fell to the floor spilling out all the contents.

She picked everything up and wiped up the glue exclaiming, "I did it! I made a big mess and cleaned it up all by myself."

We can applaud Bay's victory over her circumstances, but they happened intentionally in a loving, caring culture. Great gains happen when we create a culture that meets physical, social, and emotional needs and builds relationships. Bay is an example of what we must do for every student to have hope for a better future, so they can learn. We've got to touch our students' hearts before we can reach their minds. Bay felt she belonged. Inclusion activities built Bay's confidence. Maslow in action.

EVERYONE NEEDS A WARRIOR

As educators, we face innumerable situations and experiences we never dreamed imaginable. You can't make this stuff up. It's an honor to be part of our learners' lives and stories. The following examples are such.

Being a warrior for kids started when I began my first teaching job in Germany with the Department of Defense. My first year of teaching was a wild roller coaster ride. I'm still amazed that I wasn't so dented that I dropped out to find a new calling.

My first year, I taught sixth grade. One day after school, a shy girl confided, "I've been thinking about what you tell us every day—to believe in ourselves and that we can be anything we want to be with effort, help, and belief in ourselves. You believe in us. I want more for my life and my sisters. My dad does things to us." I listened to her story as tears streamed down her face, and I held back my own. She shared her deep, dark secret hoping for a better life-—hoping to break free from her bondage. She was only 12.

I stoically reported her dad to the school counselor and Child Protective Services—it's what I'm required to do. My heart still hurts from this experience when I learned that sometimes justice isn't really justice. I was summoned to court. I fought for *my* girl, but she had to move out of her home. She had to leave her family, and she wasn't the offender. In the end, her dad received an 18- year prison sentence—long enough for her youngest sister to reach age 18. However, I felt my sweet girl, my brave student, lost. We lost. I lost. Why did she get shipped off to a girls' home separated from her sisters?

When we're a warrior for our students, we don't always get our desired outcome. Don't ever stop trying. Be their warrior anyway.

Then there was the time that same year. A colonel scheduled a conference with me because his "gifted" daughter received a C on her report card. Literally shaking in my shoes and trying not to stutter during our conference, I mustered confidence sharing work samples to back my statements. Stating, "Sir, she did not produce quality work. She knew what was expected and chose not to meet the requirements." His daughter finally fessed up to not doing the assignments with excellence. After the conference, she learned to rise above and beyond being "gifted" and give everything her best shot. She became a student who led others to deeper thinking and learning, and she strived to do her best instead of trying to slide by. It was never about the grade. It was about living up to her full potential. When we have high expectations for *all* our students and help them reach them, we're their warriors.

Also, that first year, I learned one of my 12-year-old students was an alcoholic. How could this be? She was just a baby to me. I signed up to teach kids the basics, you know, like the three R's. I didn't realize teaching would include so much social work. Boy, was I naive. With the help of the school counselor and the right resources, she entered a recovery program. At the time, I just did what I had to do so that she would have a successful life, not realizing that I was her warrior.

My first year of teaching was far from successful. Once, my sixth graders were so loud and out of control that I tried drama to grab their attention during a math lesson. For whatever reason, I leaped up on a table to get their attention. Not a stellar move on my part and certainly nothing I'd ever learned in my classroom management training, but I was desperate. CRASH! THUMP! To my dismay, this approach totally backfired. The table cracked in half. I stumbled and bumbled to the floor in a ta-da pose, causing me to lose even more control of the class as they all drummed their fingers on their legs and sang, "Nah, nah, nah, nah... pop goes the table." Ugh. Epic fail.

I made more mistakes than anyone can count (I still do), but in the midst of my learning curve and failures, I was a warrior for at least three students whose stories I shared. So was I truly a failure? Hopefully, this inspires you. Never give up. Even on your worst day, someone needs you to believe in them and advocate for them.

I've worked with colonels' kids and kids from poverty-stricken families and everything in between. No matter what a student's background and ability, they all have one thing in common: to be treated equally with opportunities that stretch them to be better. They all want to belong, contribute, and be loved. They *all* need someone to be their warrior!

 "Every child deserves a champion—an adult who will never give up on them, who understands the power of connection, and insists that they become the best that they can possibly be."

— RITA F. PIERSON

HOW TO USE THIS BOOK

While this is written in first-person narrative style and packed with real-life stories from my elementary teaching (Pre-K through six) experience, it's truly more about you and how you apply the principles to make a difference for *all* students. The stories are simply an illustration of how I've applied them to provide concrete examples and results. These stories also remind us that our words and actions have the power to transform lives.

This book has three main sections: Culture, Community, and Be STRONG. Each principle incorporates a relevant story of how the principle is applied with real-life results and why it is important. The chapters that follow each principle are doable strategies for bringing the principle to life for your learners. It isn't a step-by-step "how-to" book. It's about timeless principles you weave into what you are already doing that can change *every* student's trajectory. Each chapter ends with personal reflection questions and ways to connect with a community of warriors.

I hope that something in this book sparks you to keep going and keep doing what is best for *all* kids because what you do is hard. It is exhausting, but it's worth it.

We all have moments, seasons, even minutes that make us or break us. Let's ensure that kids have multiple moments, plentiful people, and a surplus of seasons that shape them to be champions.

Let's do it! Let's be purposeful and intentional with the principles outlined in this book. Jump all in or take baby steps—just do something more today than you did yesterday to *be their warrior.*

PRINCIPLE 1: CULTURE

Creating a positive culture is the foundation for building unwavering relationships and high student achievement.

"The time you spend building a positive culture is never wasted—It is time invested."

— UNKNOWN

The first day of school was glorious—better than the honeymoon stage of a new class. My first graders were filled with inquiry and kindness. They listened intently to lessons and worked well together. Everything worked smoothly just like a Pinterest classroom photo. Then, day two arrived. That's when Zach walked through the door and upset the proverbial apple cart. He entered the room screaming and wailing like a dog that got its paw stuck in a trap. The children looked at him with bewilderment. My heart skipped a beat as I thought about what my day was going to look like. Did I have the stamina for this?

Next, he ran laps around and around the carpeted gathering area, followed by bouts of spinning on his head. Then he told me he was hungry. From that day on, part of his arrival routine was to eat extra snacks on top of the school-provided breakfast. He had been deprived of food sometime during his 6-year-old life. I met that need and 100s and 100s of others. No exaggeration. He challenged me every single day to think outside-of-the-box for him to succeed. One day, I even sat under a table with him to listen to him read since he refused to come out. Hey, the mission was accomplished—he read (and yes, I still had 22 other tiny human needs to meet without an aide.)

Zach had experienced more trauma than any person should have to endure, especially a vulnerable 6-year-old. The month before he stepped through our classroom door, he witnessed his mom's death and the imprisonment of his dad. I'd like to tell you everything turned around quickly and gloriously but it didn't. However, slow and steady always wins the race. Through building a relationship with him, listening to his needs and meeting them, and creating a positive, caring culture with predictable structure and consistency, he went from being a non-reader who climbed on the counters, screamed, and threw furniture to a student who was able to read on grade level by the end of the year. He accomplished five growth levels; that's astounding growth in "normal" circumstances, let alone a child who had just experienced intense trauma. He also became a contributing member of our class, joining in all morning meetings. All this growth didn't come without a plan and being intentional. In fact, I accessed every resource at my disposal to get others involved in meeting his needs. I could have thrown my hands up in the air and just shrugged with defeat and chatted with colleagues about how awful he behaved and his unstable home life. It certainly would have been easier. However, I chose to take action for his sake.

With my administration's support, we came up with a purposeful plan that involved the school bookkeeper and custodian. They were his warriors too. You don't have to do it alone. In fact, it's daunting to meet every child's needs alone. Once you know a child's needs, get others involved.

Zach's purposeful plan involved the following strategies but wasn't limited to them. In fact, sometimes, strategies for him were implemented on-the-spot according to his needs.

PURPOSEFUL PLAN- STRATEGIES THAT CAN BE USED FOR *ALL* LEARNERS

- Visual schedule that was divided into the different parts of his day.
- A self-monitoring scale by each part of his day. (Some people call this "chunking.") It included visual reminders such as a smiley face, straight face, and frowning face corresponding to each time period/activity. Zach chose these faces to self regulate in the future. A smiley face for when he had followed through without receiving redirection. A straight face for needing redirection during that chunk of time. A frowning face for needing redirection more than three times. I don't like smiley faces and frowns, but Zach chose this system. The frown was explained as a need for improvement, not as doing something bad.
- A reward system was implemented with increasing expectations as Zach achieved greater success. With incentives of Zach's choice, which reinforced the desired behavior, I was able to scale back, and the behavior became a habit. At that point rewards and verbal praise are still essential but don't have to be unyielding. Remember: It's important to reinforce desired behavior quickly and consistently with a tangible reward every time they do the desired behavior. Reinforcers need to be rewarded almost immediately when the desired behavior is demonstrated. Consistency is key to constructive change and desired

outcomes. When one behavior is modified, move onto another using the same method.

- Established a check-in system. My assistant principal checked in on him three times a day. She rewarded him at the end of each day when he earned his reward. The reward was either tangible or intangible like undivided time with the assistant principal. If he didn't earn his reward, she modeled what he should do to improve.

- Established a system for him to take frequent breaks throughout the day. Zach was sent to the office throughout the day to visit and assist the school bookkeeper. The breaks prevented full-blown meltdowns and established a positive relationship with the bookkeeper. It also allowed me to have a break so that I could be my best for him.

- Set up a system for him to assist the custodian after he ate his lunch. This kept him engaged and enabled him to establish a relationship with her. (She was a grandmother figure to him.) Zach struggled with transitions, so this system helped him work with her and transition back to the classroom well.

- Miracle Cube Timer. He was taught to set the timer for five minutes and unpack his belongings and begin his school day before the timer went off. He loved to beat the timer. This strategy enabled him to focus on putting his belongings away rather than run around the classroom. The timer was also useful for completing chunks of work. He had to do so many minutes of work, and then he could take a break. I love the miracle cube timer because it is self-regulating. Once you teach a student how to use it, they can be autonomous.

As stated earlier, there were many, many strategies used to help Zach succeed, but these are a few that can work for all students when you adapt them to your specific students' needs. In chapter 2, I share ways to assess students' needs. After you know the antecedent to their behavior, craft a prescribed plan. Being intentional guides you to be their warrior, and you'll see them soar.

As I championed for Zach throughout the year and through what felt like endless meetings, I reminded myself of the following quote: "*Those who are hardest to love need it the most.*"— Socrates

> "Building a culture of excellence is collaborative."

By being his warrior and not giving up on him, no matter how he behaved, he changed. I changed too. As with every challenging student, Zach made me a better teacher; I had to learn new methods. I spent so much time and energy thinking about helping him that he wiggled his way into my heart. Forever.

On the last day of school, he wanted to hold my hand as I walked everyone to their bus. He looked me in the eye and pleaded, "Will you please go with me to second grade?" I cried as I reassured him that he was ready, and I'd still be available for him. I truly loved him. He was challenging, but I was his warrior, and he knew it.

I continue to follow up with him. Although he still has many of his challenges, the foundation we built through establishing a positive culture and following the principles and strategies that I share put him on a positive and confident path. Socially, he is now bright and brilliant instead of cowering under a table or throwing furniture. Building a caring culture and putting kids first always wins.

Cultivating a positive culture is the foundation for building relationships leading to high student achievement. The Oxford Dictionary defines culture as "the attitudes and behavior characteristics of a particular social group." When I talk about classroom or school culture, I am talking about the environment and what we physically do to create a caring climate with positive attitudes and behavior. A thriving culture is creating a positive environment for the interactions we have with students, staff, and colleagues. Our culture is established through how we work together, talk together, treat each other, the lessons we plan and facilitate, and emotional connections.

Relationships are the core of a caring culture. It takes time and intentionality to create connections. Relationships are best cultivated in an environment filled with the strategies (actions you take) in this principle, Culture.

In the second principle, we'll explore how to cement relationships yielding high student achievement.

According to multiple studies done by a wide array of researchers, students who are at both affluent and below poverty levels have higher achievement when the culture is right for learning (Walker, n.d.). Additionally, there is "substantial evidence that positive school climates contribute to academic achievement and can improve outcomes for students, especially those from lower socioeconomic backgrounds"(Walker, n.d.).

So how do you establish that kind of culture meeting physiological, safety, love, belonging, and esteem needs when so many of our students come with needs far greater than we can imagine?

> **"Relationships are the core of a caring culture."**

Begin by setting the tone and creating a positive, caring culture that fosters loving relationships. Apply the strategies in the following chapters to your current situation. Sounds easy, right? Most teachers naturally strive to have a positive culture. However, intentionally devoting time to these strategies and incorporating them effectively and efficiently leads to a culture that supports *all* students' success.

SET THE TONE

Setting the right tone creates a culture for success.

Set the tone for a positive, caring culture by creating an impactful impression and establishing the feeling, pace, attitude, and mood expressing who you are, what you value, and what it means to be a member of your classroom or school.

A thermometer reacts to its environment. A thermostat sets it. We are our students' thermostat. We set the culture, and they react to it.

GREET & FAREWELL DAILY

Greeting students at the door every day is a powerful way to create a positive culture. Make a big deal of their arrival! Daily, I greeted everyone with a smile and a "bee kiss"—a stuffed bee kissed my students on the cheek to help them "bee" the best they can be. Yeah, can you tell I taught first grade? Students reminded me if I forgot to give them a "bee kiss"; they looked forward to it. If a student was crying or had a grumpy look on their face, their needs were addressed before the day began. This simple act sets the tone for the day, promotes a sense of belonging, and gives students the social and emotional support needed to help them feel invested in their learning.

Please remember: It's all about the heart. Kids instinctively know if you are sincere or not. So it doesn't matter if it's a "bee kiss," a dance, a high five, or a special handshake. The greeting can be as simple as standing at the door saying "hi" with a smile. What matters is your attitude. The purpose is to make a personal connection with each student every day. The bottom line is this: It's not the technique. It's the care and connection behind what you do. Do you *really* care for kids—*all* of them? There is no technique you can implement that will work unless you truly care. Look them in the eye and let them know you're on their side. It begins with a greeting.

Greeting time is powerful when you listen to kids' stories and connect with them. It truly limits behavior challenges later. "In a recent study, positive greetings at the classroom door increased students' academic engagement by 20% and decreased disruptive classroom behavior by 9%"(Terada, 2018). So set a positive tone with a smile and a greeting. Kids love it.

> "Greet students at the door to make a personal connection. It's not the technique. It's the care and connection behind what you do."

There is significant emphasis placed on greeting students at the door. For a good reason. But what about saying goodbye to them at the door or bus? It's just as important to say goodbye to students when developing a positive, caring culture. Think about all the cultures in the world. Every last one of them has salutations and farewells. Goodbyes at the end of the day are just as crucial as greetings at the beginning of the day.

When students depart for the day (or class period), tell them you can't wait until you see them tomorrow. Sometimes this can be difficult to say to challenging kids, but when you believe in them and love them, eventually they become less challenging. Stand at the door and say, "Goodbye, have a wonderful day." Be sure to tell them something good they did for that day. This ends their day on a positive note giving them a reason to return.

I waved goodbye to students using the American Sign Language sign for "I love you" at the bus ramp. I stumbled upon doing this by accident. It all started when one of my students who had a history of high absenteeism landed in my class. Determined he wouldn't keep that record in my class, I thought of creative ways to let him know he was valued and important. One way was as follows: I told him to look out the bus window for me—I'd wave at him. Then I told him I couldn't wait until I saw him in the morning. This worked. He looked out the window for me and waved in return with a huge smile plastered across his face. He came to school more than ever. So be sure to say goodbye to your students too.

These strategies also apply to adults. When I lead a professional development session, I stand at the door and greet everyone as they come through the door. I love watching their body language change from tense to surprised as they return a smile. When I stand at the door and say, "Have a great day," they leave happy. I've attended many conferences where, more often than not, no one greets you. I've also attended some where I'm greeted. Guess which one makes me feel at ease and ready to learn and listen? You got it—greeting at the door.

5 SIMPLE WAYS TO GREET STUDENTS

1. Use their name—Calling someone by name creates a connection.
2. Make a request—Asking them to do something specific gives them a sense of purpose.
3. Ask your students how they want to be greeted and *do* what they suggest.

4. Ask a question. Follow up with what a student told you the day before that they'd be doing. For example: "How was your baseball game?"

5. Use gestures such as a thumbs-up, smile, special handshake, dance, etc.

These strategies apply to all learners. Be intentional about creating a positive culture by setting the tone with a greeting and farewell.

MORNING MEETING & TEAM BUILDING

To further build culture, conduct a morning meeting to build relation-ships with each other through sharing and team building. This is important for resource teachers too. I'm a STEM (Science, Technology, Engineering, & Mathematics) teacher now. So, I take my own advice, and I program 5-10 minutes of a morning meeting rendition for every class. It's imperative to build culture first. Then, the lesson.

One morning in my first-grade class, I used an oral language sentence starter for the morning meeting. I wasn't emotionally prepared for my children's burdens that seemed as everyday-ordinary to them as breathing and getting dressed. My heart was forever changed. I hope I never forget the heavy loads my kids bear. That morning, I said, "Finish this sentence: I feel afraid when...." I was expecting to hear things like: "I feel afraid when I see spiders." But no —my kids said, "I feel afraid when I'm left alone in the car watching the baby." They are six! "I feel afraid when my parents fight." "I feel afraid when my mom says I have to leave home and never come back." "I get nervous when dad leaves," and the list went on and on as they poured out their fears. As we calmly chatted, I reassured them, and we grew closer emotionally from sharing.

I've always loved the quote by Teresa Kwant: "*Be the teacher who when given the 'hard' class says, These aren't the hard kids, these are my kids."*

These *hard* kids were *my* kids. I was reminded that their brains and bodies were tense with anxiety, causing them to be hard to deal with. Please remember children today live in a myriad of traumatic situations such as divorce, death, absentee guardians, domestic violence, abuse (psychological, physical, sexual, emotional), parental incarceration, etc. Therefore, it's important to be empathetic to the circumstances that children are in. We need to help them overcome the effects of those situations to engage in the learning environment fully. A relaxed brain is a learning brain. Building a safe, loving, nurturing culture is paramount to their success and security.

Really listen to them. Tune in. Listen to their stories. Celebrate diversity. Often when students are talking to me, I'm doing what seems like twenty other tasks, so I give them a courtesy nod like I am listening—but I'm too distracted to hear their heart. I *know* I need to be fully present, but it is so hard to do with demands piled on top of demands. However, during the morning meeting, I intentionally sit with my class and give them my undivided attention focusing on their needs. During the morning meeting, sit with your students and give them 100% of your attention. They need it. They'll love you for it. So, just through a simple morning meeting, a caring culture is built on trust and love.

Some mornings we play games like rock, paper, scissors, or we do a team-building activity like creating a plastic cup pyramid, or we greet each other with kind words and a high five,

> "A relaxed brain is a learning brain. Building a safe, loving, nurturing culture is paramount to student success and security."

which I role model, so they see and hear how to interact with one another. The following ideas are some of my students' favorites, and they can be implemented in your class to fit your students' needs.

MORNING MEETING AND TEAM BUILDING ACTIVITIES

- **Hit the Floor**—This is a chant that goes like this: "1,2,3,4 come on (insert student's name) hit the floor. We're so glad you're here today. Hooray. Hooray. Hooray!" Here's how it works: Circle up on a carpeted area. The student whose name is called goes to the center of the circle and does a movement or dance unique to them. They must go back to the circle by the time everyone chants the last hooray. Repeat until everyone has had a turn.
- **Simply share a sentence** of something on your mind. Share something you are anxious about, happy about, looking forward to, etc.
- **Good Things**—This is a quick and easy activity for nearly every age. Each student turns to one of their neighbors and tells them something good. The "good thing" can be as simple as eating something they liked for dinner last night. The following "talking stems" are helpful: One good thing in my life is . . . Something good that happened is . . .
- **Name Alliteration**—Students create an adjective or verb to go before their name. Example: Good morning (or afternoon), I'm Marvelous Maddox, Active Alice, etc. (Some students have fun adding multiple adjectives that have alliteration.)
- **It All Adds Up**—This combines math and greetings into one! The teacher prepares several flashcards for this activity: one set will have math problems, and the other set will have the answers. Mix up the cards and have students each choose one. They then have to find the student who holds the match to solve the problem and greet each other! This greeting is a great one to grow throughout the year. Students can start super simple, and as they advance in

their studies of math, the problems can get harder to solve (Jagodowski, n.d.). Use math facts that work for your group such as add, subtract, multiply, divide, time, money, fractions, etc.

At the secondary level, I'd have students sit in a circle and do a simple check in. You can explain that understanding how everyone is checking into the space allows for empathy and understanding. For example, I might say, "I'm checking in happy and nervous today. I'm happy to be with all of you but nervous because I've never taught the lesson we're going to do today, and I don't know how it will go. How are you checking in? Are you sad, calm, cautious, excited, etc.?" The purpose of checking in and morning meetings is creating a positive, caring environment and to build trust, communication, and community.

Google morning meeting if these ideas don't fit your needs. There are 100s of ideas. Just ensure you incorporate morning meetings to build a culture of care and collaboration. Truly anything that gets your learners talking, making connections, and creating community is worth five to ten minutes every day.

If you think you don't have time for greeting students at the door and a morning meeting, you'll have to make time to diffuse and discipline behavior challenges later.

Creating a positive, caring culture diminishes behavior challenges because students have a sense of belonging and rise to class expectations.

The following are some suggested norms or protocols for children for communicating during morning meetings.

8 *KEY* COMMUNICATION SKILLS TO UNPACK WITH CHILDREN BEFORE SHARING STORIES.

1. Let everyone have a turn at speaking.
2. Don't make fun of other people's ideas; be respectful.
3. Listen to others when it's their turn. Listening to others is how we learn.
4. Take time to talk about and explore new ideas.
5. Ask questions of others and listen carefully to their answers.
6. Don't be afraid to speak up; your voice matters.
7. If you don't agree with someone, that's okay, but don't carry the argument with you into other activities.
8. Be kind, be friendly, be interested, be respectful, and have fun! (Educate2Empower, n.d.)

WHAT ARE YOU HOLDING ONTO THAT MIGHT NOT CONTRIBUTE TO THE CULTURE YOU WANT?

I ditched the job chart. I found it difficult to remember to update and manage. Also, I found it didn't contribute to creating a positive, caring culture—quite the contrary. Students argued about who was the line leader, who held the door, and who sharpened pencils. You name it. This behavior was annoying and counterproductive.

So what do I do? Each morning, I draw a new student's name to be "King or Queen" for the day. I have a huge, sparkling, bejeweled crown displayed at the front of the class.

> "What practice are you holding onto out of habit that doesn't contribute to the culture you want to create?"

Whoever is the king or queen for the day has their name posted under the crown. They do every job needed for the day. They're literally the king or queen for the day. They even get to choose others to help them do jobs. There is no more arguing about who does what job, and students take ownership and responsibility.

It might not be a job chart, but what practice are you holding onto out of habit that doesn't contribute to the culture you want to create? Remember, you set the tone. Removing something counterproductive to your culture packs a powerful punch in creating a positive, caring culture where everyone, regardless of background or ability, shines.

NEXT STEPS:

1. To begin setting the tone, ask yourself: How do I want my students to feel when they arrive? How do I want my students to feel when they are in my class? How do I want students to feel when they leave? Be intentional about making your answers happen.
2. What will you do tomorrow that you may not already be doing to set a positive tone for the day?
3. What else can you do to set the tone for *all* students to succeed? (Not just the challenging ones, but for sure the challenging ones.)

CONNECT:

We all aspire to create a positive culture for our students. Connect with other warrior teachers and share what you do on Twitter or Instagram. **Share how you set the tone and the results.** Your stories and pictures may be just what someone needs for encouragement to be a warrior for their students. You make a difference. Let's create a community, a movement amplifying *all* students. Use the hashtag #BeTheirWarrior.

2

ASSESS ALL STUDENTS' NEEDS

Create a culture that allows for ongoing informal assessment of students' needs.

*W*ouldn't it be crazy to visit the doctor for a sore throat, and the doctor prescribed a muscle relaxer for your back? If the doctor doesn't observe you, examine you, and ask some questions, they won't know what to prescribe correctly. The same is true with your students. You've got to talk with them. Observe them. Ask questions and learn about them, so you have a feel for their needs. Much of that is done through the morning meeting, greeting and farewelling, and interacting like a classroom family. Once you've established those routines as part of your culture, each student's story is embedded in your mind.

Knowing their stories gives you information to determine their needs. Those needs usually boil down to the following categories: social, emotional, physical, and academic. Once you know the needs, you access every resource at your disposal. Make a plan and become intentional about meeting those needs. While we have limited influence on students' home lives, we can adapt our environment, interactions, and instruction to change their lives positively.

IT'S NOT WORTH YOUR TIME. OR IS IT?

Knowing students' needs is one thing. Advocating for them is another. For some, championing for all students' needs comes easily. For others, it may seem like a waste of time. I know it wasn't a waste of time for a first-year teacher, but her mentor advised her otherwise. The following story illustrates how knowing your students' needs provides a framework for success.

January, halfway through the year, the new graduate, Josie, took over a second-grade class. She was brand new to everything, including the Response To Intervention (RTI) process. Josie was passionate about teaching and learning. She was passionate about making her class a fun place to learn and meet every student's needs. After a short while, she discovered one of her students needed more assistance to learn than she could provide. She informed her mentor teacher of the student's needs. Her mentor teacher advised her not to take the time to get the student help through the RTI process, which is the standard way to get additional help at her school. She reasoned that there wasn't enough time to get the student help because the process would take until the end of the school year. She also informed Josie that her student would be overlooked because he had average grades. They needed to start with the RTI process at their school, and then if there were no significant gains, the student wouldn't be considered for other options. Josie knew her student inside and out from listening to him and getting to know him and his needs.

I'm not faulting her mentor teacher. It makes sense it would take time, and Josie wouldn't reap the benefits. To most, it's logical and not worth the effort. Thankfully, Josie followed her gut instinct and followed her belief in doing whatever it takes to help a student succeed. She went through the RTI process advocating for her student who she knew needed more assistance for his success. A person is more than a grade. He needed social skills and help with inferring. After the RTI process, the student was formally tested. A team learned from the testing results that the student needed extra support. Josie built a relationship, performed ongoing informal assessments of emotions and academics, and got her student the needed help.

Even though Josie didn't get the extra support in her class for the student, she advocated for him to have extra support during his next

> **"Persistent passion equals results."**

school year. What if she hadn't gone through the process? He'd have to wait another whole year before getting the help and support needed to succeed. Thankfully, Josie didn't let him slip through the cracks. We've got to trust our gut and go through the process. No matter what. Persistent passion equals results. It's not about us and the help we get. It's all about our students and their needs.

EVALUATING EMOTIONAL NEEDS

Assessing students' needs involves some "gut work." You know your kids best. Trust your instincts. They'll guide you toward students' needs. There is no standardized test for that. The responsibility of meeting each and every need is overwhelming. It can be done, though, with a plan and purpose.

There isn't a one-size-fits-all solution to meeting students' needs. For example, I had a student who had multiple meltdowns. My student teacher looked at me with hopeful eyes and questioned, "What are you going to do?" I shrugged, "I don't know yet. I've got to get to know him." It probably wasn't the answer he was looking for from an award-winning teacher. After all, shouldn't I have *all* the answers?

You see, sometimes we don't have *all* the answers when we feel like we're supposed to. It's okay not to know. That's why building relationships are key. It takes time to analyze our students' triggers that led up to undesirable behavior. We have to study our students. How can we know what to do without ongoing informal assessment? The following story highlights informal assessment.

On the second day of first grade, JJ had a screaming meltdown. In anger, he threw a stool and started slinging objects across the classroom. To keep the other 22 first graders safe, I assisted JJ to the floor, helping him take slow breaths and calm down. (What a sight that must have been all while wearing a skirt that almost ended up around my ears.) My student teacher was taking mental notes on how I solved the problem and met JJ's needs. I didn't really meet JJ's needs that day. I did de-escalate a meltdown. All I knew was he had a *fight or flight* reaction to almost every situation. I needed time to learn JJ. In time, I learned his triggers. I learned new environments and new expectations led to meltdowns. Any change in routine led to meltdowns. All transitions led to meltdowns. JJ hadn't learned how to cope with overstimulation and change. I had to get to know him and use my gut instincts to come up with ways to avoid the triggers and ways to respond to triggers.

When we build relationships with our students' best interests in mind, it's easier to assess their emotional needs and come up with solutions. Sometimes, most times, there isn't a textbook answer. We also need to take note of the antecedent to undesired behaviors to prescribe a plan fitting the student and their behavior. You'll know your students' needs once you are intentional about learning their needs. Use your creative gut instincts about how to implement a strategy for your student. If you can't think of a solution, ask. I've asked 100s and 100s of educators for help. (More on meeting needs in the following chapters.)

Document, document, document. Document triggers. Document

antecedents. Document every intervention and its results. It's time-consuming, I know. But data helps determine a corrective path. Document every parent conference. Document every resource you've consulted. Documentation helps you analyze your students' emotional needs. The more documentation that you have, the higher the likelihood of getting additional help for a student that needs it. For example, one year, I had a parent ask me to list all the interventions I'd been doing without a 504 plan or I.E.P. (Individualized Instructional Plan) for her son. When I compiled the list for her, I was as stunned as her. It was two double-spaced typed pages. Because I had a positive relationship with her and her child, the data was convincing. Prior, she was reluctant to seek help. After, she cried and opened up and sought help. The result was a better education and future for her son, who needed specialized help. None of that would have been possible without documentation.

Remember to continually consider all students' emotional wellbeing.(Social Emotional Learning - SEL) How are they feeling? Are they hurting emotionally? When we see someone hurting because of their environment, it isn't easy on our eyes, but we are moved with compassion, a deep stirring inside us to do something different. Their hurt causes us to take action.

Once you know kids' needs, examine your practice. Are you meeting them, or are you blaming parents, the system, testing, etc.? I get it. I've been there. Oftentimes, our system doesn't support us with one more challenging student and one more mandate. What we need are more hands and resources to set students up for success and life. However, over time, my attitude, desire, and skills evolved because I became intentional about doing everything possible to make a difference. If I couldn't help a student, I found someone with the skills that could. After assessing and identifying your students' needs, chase

> "Document, document, document. Documentation helps you analyze your students' emotional needs."

down ways to meet them. Constantly and intentionally be fearless, advocating for the needs of all kids.

ASSESS LEARNING NEEDS OF *ALL* LEARNERS

There are essentially two reasons the assessment of student learning is important: 1. Improvement. Improving your lessons and student improvement. 2. Finding ways to help all students grow and succeed. When you know their challenges, you can formulate a plan to overcome them. If you don't assess, you waste valuable teaching time on what is already mastered.

"Asking students to demonstrate their understanding of subject matter is critical to the learning process; it is essential to evaluate whether the lessons' educational goals and standards are being met. Assessment is an integral part of instruction" (Person, 2008). For me, much of my effective assessment is done informally, or it's performance-based. Assessment is ongoing. Minute by minute, day by day, and summative upon summative. All forms of assessment give a complete picture of a student's needs.

I'll never forget when I was an intern. I was given the task of administering a bubble-in-the-answer standardized reading test to a second-grader. One of the questions sought initial consonant knowledge by asking which picture started with the letter "h." The options were pictures of a donkey, horse, cat, and dog. The student selected the donkey. I was puzzled. I was sure he knew his initial consonant sounds. I inquired, "What made you select that picture?" Beaming with pride because he *just knew* he'd gotten it right, he replied, pointing to the donkey, "That right there is a honkey." So if I'd never inquired, I would have thought he didn't know initial consonants. He was just confused with what to call animals, which is a totally different lesson. Authentic, performance-based assessment gives insight into students' needs far better than any standardized test. Know your students.

Assessment allows us to move all students forward no matter what they need.

We all know this as educators, but it's so important it's worth repeating. Assessing all students' individual needs, and creating a plan to meet them is a *huge* piece of the puzzle of strategies to being their warrior. We need to know for equity. We need to know, so no student slides by or slips through the cracks. We need to know, so we know not just *what* to teach them, but *how* to teach them. Everyone learns in different ways and requires different methods and mediums. So we've got to know our students on an emotional, personal, and academic level. We've got to know them as a total, wonderful human package and then aspire to meet their needs and coach them through the process.

One beautiful way to document growth over time and assess student progress is through keeping a portfolio for each student. Portfolios are a wonderful way to show growth and areas to work on to families during conferences. Portfolios are useful for student-led conferences. I always loved visiting each student's portfolio at the end of each quarter, because the evidence in the portfolio was clear. The work samples revealed areas where students made tremendous growth, and they clearly pointed me to areas to develop.

★ **Try this:**
- Create a folder for each student to collect work samples. (I like to put them in a hanging file.) It's a portfolio of their work. (Digital portfolios are a great tool to guide instruction and celebrate student work.)
- Collect work samples from each subject area at predetermined intervals to see growth and areas to work on. (Be sure to have a baseline sample for each area.) I love looking back at these. I'm often so focused on growth, I forget how far students have come until I visit their portfolios and have physical evidence.
- Allow students to choose what goes into their portfolio.
- Have students look at their portfolio to see their growth and progress and determine areas to work on. Have them set goals.
- Use rubrics. Communicate clear expectations for each area on the rubric.
- As you walk around the room daily, write your informal observations on Post-It notes. Stick those in the portfolios. When you pull out the portfolio, you have a lot of formal and informal data to determine the best action plan for each student.

Regardless of their socioeconomic background, our students come to us with needs: physical, social, emotional, and academic. When we assess their needs by building a culture rooted in relationships, we'll know better how to meet them. We level the learning playing field when we meet *all* our students' needs. When their needs are met, high academic achievement is a byproduct. It doesn't matter if a student comes from an affluent family. They may crave adult attention. It doesn't matter if a student comes from a poverty-stricken family; they may need shoes that fit to concentrate on the lesson instead of foot pain that feels like a crab pinching their toes. No matter the need, find out about it and fill it.

NEXT STEPS:

1. Remember, there's no one-size-fits-all solution, strategy, method, or answer for meeting students' needs. We need to meet *all* students' needs right where they're at and figure out what works best for each one to be their warrior. It starts with a relationship. What can you do tomorrow to get to know your students better?
2. Assessment is all about learning and meeting student needs; when we know their needs, we can develop a plan to meet all students' needs. What can you do tomorrow/this week to assess your students' social, emotional, physical, and academic needs?
3. How will you (and a support team) devise a plan to meet them? You're not alone.

CONNECT:

Connect with other warrior teachers and share what you do on Twitter or Instagram. **Share how you assessed your students' social,** emotional, physical, and academic needs. **Share the results. Share how you build relationships.** Your stories and pictures may be just what someone needs for encouragement to be a warrior for their students. You make a difference. Let's create a community, a movement amplifying *all* students. Use the hashtag #BeTheirWarrior.

3

CREATE A CULTURE THAT SUPPORTS PHYSICAL NEEDS

Create a caring culture that meets *all* students' basic physical needs.

*W*hat do students' physical needs have to do with creating a positive, caring culture? Everything. Creating a culture meeting all students' physical needs seems as common sense as learning their names. But it's more complex than decorations and furniture. In fact, it's the foundation for bonding relationships.

According to Maslow, we can't build lasting relationships that lead to learning until we meet all students' physiological and safety needs. Let's break that down by asking the following question: Are your students getting "all of their basic physical needs met? These basic needs include food, water, sleep, oxygen, and warmth" (Kline, n.d.).

Our school has a clothes closet that provides shoes, coats, and clothes for students. The items are donated by community members or staff. Students who come to school with clothing or hygiene needs may go to the nurse to meet those needs. If you don't have a school system to meet these needs, you can start a clothing and hygiene closet. You are the one that makes the difference.

Evaluate physical needs: Are their shoes too small? Too big? Do they need a coat? Are they getting proper sleep and nutrition? Sleep deprivation leads to defiant behavior.

Most parents think their children are getting enough sleep but are bewildered when their child's behavior is less than desirable. They are puzzled by their child's plummeting academic achievement. What's the epidemic? Lack of sleep. For real. It's a simple thing that needs to be remedied. It's a little thing that makes a *huge* difference in improving a child's state of mind, thereby improving their behavior and academic performance.

During a parent conference, a dad asked me how much sleep a 6-year-old needed. I said, "About nine hours a night. I really don't know. Let's Google it."

We looked it up together. The results dropped the parent's jaw. In astonishment, he stated, "9-12 hours. Really? That means I have to put my child to bed at 7:30 PM."

"Yep!"

"What about sports?"

I replied, "Do you want them to have proper rest to grow and thrive academically? They need sleep to concentrate." I, too, throw tantrums when I haven't had enough sleep. (Sure, they look different from a child-like meltdown, but they happen. Unfortunately. Just ask my husband.) The world appears bleaker when I'm sleep deprived. When I'm tired, I'm not at my best. I might respond with a snappy tone of voice. My patience isn't as polished. It's the same for our kids.

With his discovery, the parent made me realize the importance of informing everyone about proper sleep. (It can improve a multitude of challenges. Just one physical need met changes everything.)

So what does the American Academy of Pediatrics say is the proper amount of sleep?

American Academy of Pediatrics recommends the following sleep hours:

- Infants 4 months to 12 months should sleep 12 to 16 hours per 24 hours (including naps) regularly to promote optimal health.
- Children 1 to 2 years of age should sleep 11 to 14 hours per 24 hours (including naps) regularly to promote optimal health.
- Children 3 to 5 years of age should sleep 10 to 13 hours per 24 hours (including naps) regularly to promote optimal health.
- Children 6 to 12 years of age should sleep 9 to 12 hours per 24 hours regularly to promote optimal health.
- Teenagers 13 to 18 years of age should sleep 8 to 10 hours per 24 hours regularly to promote optimal health (Paruthi & Brooks, 2016).

Adequate sleep duration regularly leads to improved attention, behavior, learning, memory, emotional regulation, quality of life, and mental and physical health. Not getting enough sleep each night is associated with increased injuries, hypertension, obesity, and depression, especially for teens who may experience an increased risk of self-harm or suicidal thoughts.

 Try This:

1. Share with families the American Academy of Pediatrics recommended sleep guidelines.
2. Inform families the benefits of a *no electronics two hours before bed policy* so students can blissfully fall asleep.
3. Inform families the benefits of no devices in the bedroom during the night. (Studies show students are sleep deprived because they're up all night on a screen. Screens aren't the problem. Time, place, and duration are.)

If students aren't getting their basic physical needs met, they can't learn. I'm sure you are already finding creative ways to meet your students' basic needs. The following are some I've done.

Let students bring a water bottle. Let them have a drink whenever they need it. I used to not let students have water bottles at their desks or tables at any one time. I didn't like the mess. One day, I realized they needed to leave class more often to get a drink, which resulted in time off task. Besides, I thought about how I function when I'm in a class. I always bring my water bottle and a snack. Our students are no different than we are. Let them bring their water. They will sip away and still be engaged. And the mess, well, students clean it up. I set expectations such as only allowing water. We also decide together where the water bottle will live and when they can get a drink. For example, they may not jump up in the middle of a lesson to get a drink. Other than that, they may get a drink whenever they would like. By allowing water bottles, you meet a basic physical need paving the way for better learning.

THERE'S POWER IN A SNACK BASKET

Something as simple as a snack basket packs a powerful punch in creating a positive, caring culture and meeting basic needs. Students take turns bringing in a snack to share with everyone. They quickly learn what their classroom family enjoys and work to meet their needs. How cool is that? When they bring the snack, all the students thank them.

They get to be in the spotlight of the class as they hand out the preferred snack. It's also an excellent time to instill manners. Students are expected to say, "Please" and "Thank you." I've taught students not to release what they are giving until the recipient says thank you. There are a few tug-o-wars at first, but everyone establishes the "thank you" habit. The person that delivers a snack to each and everyone for the day appears to stand a bit taller with pride. No matter who the student is, they feel special. (If a student doesn't have the means to bring in a snack, I assist them, so they have their special moment.)

How does this work? At the beginning of the year, I inform all families that we will have a snack basket, and their child will bring snacks for everyone about once a month. All families have the option to opt-out if they are unable to do this. If they opt-out, I provide snacks and let their child deliver it. No matter what, everyone gets a snack for the day. It works out great because a family sends in about 24 snacks about once a month instead of sending in a snack daily for their student. Also, this ensures that all students get a snack. It is not fun to be in a class where the students that remember a snack or their families can provide a snack are eating while others have growly tummies. The snack basket meets a basic need and builds a caring culture.

I also have a snack cupboard in my classroom for anyone that needs a snack anytime throughout the day. Often, students come without breakfast. They have a snack from the snack cupboard. So, what if you have students that aren't elementary students? Find a way to meet their need to belong, be in the spotlight, and eat a snack. When we take care of our students' basic needs, we are their warriors.

PURPOSEFUL MOVEMENT

Another physical need that students require that Maslow doesn't expound upon is purposeful movement and brain breaks. No matter a student's age, be sure that they have time to move. Some students even need to move during a lesson. I've had students pace back and forth while I delivered instructions. It wasn't a problem because they were still engaged and learning. Let them move.

Try this:

Play games like Scoot, so they move around the room to learn or gallery walks.
If you're not familiar with the game Scoot, here's how it works:

1. Scoot! is a whole-class educational game that your students will love. You may also like to do it as a station.
2. Place questions around the room. I tape the questions to the wall. I also use pictures with questions too.
3. Students have a numbered handout that corresponds to the number of questions you've placed around the room.
4. I let students use clipboards so when they move around the room, they have something to write on.
5. Next, students roam around the room answering questions or solving math problems. I don't require them to go in order. I only require that they correspond the number of the question to the number on their handout to write the answer. I require them to visit every question.
6. At the end of a set time, everyone reconvenes at their own seat.
7. You can go over the answers together or have them turn in their handouts.

One year, I had a first grader that asked if she could do her test on the floor. (Ugh, yes. I had to administer a standardized test to first graders. Not my desire.) While she took the test, she'd roll on the floor like a pencil. She'd roll away as she thought about her answer. Then, she'd roll back to the test and fill in a bubble. Roll away and think. Roll back and fill in a bubble. She did this for the entire test. Guess what? She scored the highest. So, let your students move.

Purposeful breaks consist of yoga, dancing, or for younger students: GoNoodle. GoNoodle is an organization that gets kids moving and more mindful through short, interactive videos. When these are intentionally planned to allow for physical movement, it actually resets the brain allowing for more concentration. Break time isn't a waste of time.

If you have just one particular student that needs a break out of the room, or perhaps you need a break from them, you can instill a plan I call the "Purple Folder." The purple folder serves a purpose. I've pre-arranged with a colleague or the school secretary to put an important message in the purple folder for me if they see a student show up with it. I actually don't need the message. It is just a way to give a younger student a purposeful break when otherwise they'd refuse. It works every time. The time out of the room gives the student and me a chance to breathe. Reset.

If all students have these needs met, the next stage is safety. (I don't believe these steps are like a ladder one before the other. I believe they can happen simultaneously.) How safe and secure does this student feel in their home? What about in your school, and specifically in your classroom?"

NEXT STEPS:

1. What are some physical needs that you can meet that you aren't currently meeting? How will you meet them? Who can help you?
2. Ask your students about their comfort in your classroom/school. Their answers will guide you.
3. How will you inform families of your students' physical needs lovingly?
4. No matter your students' ages, what are some ways to incorporate purposeful movement into your lesson or throughout your day?

CONNECT:

Connect with other warrior teachers and share what you do on Twitter or Instagram. **Share how you incorporate purposeful movement. Share how you handle basic student needs like water and snacks. What were the results?** Your stories and pictures may be just what someone needs for encouragement to be a warrior for their students. You make a difference. Let's create a community, a movement amplifying *all* students. Use the hashtag #BeTheirWarrior

4

CREATE A CULTURE FOR A SAFE, INVITING PHYSICAL ENVIRONMENT

Create a safe, inviting learning environment: A place and space for everyone and every type of learner.

*S*etting students up for success begins with creating a physical environment that flows well and is warm and inviting. The moment you walk in, you're embraced and wrapped in comfort like your favorite fuzzy blanket. Yet, it's active and busy with learning. It doesn't have to look like your living room or Pinterest to be inviting. It can, but it's not required. It's more important for the space to be neat, tidy, and welcoming. It's a well thought out space meeting the needs of every single learner.

Creating a physical environment conducive to learning matters. It became more evident to me than ever recently when I moved to a new school. When I entered my new classroom, I was overtaken with intense fluorescent brightness and no natural light. My new room was vast with no windows. I felt irritable. Why? The bright fake lights. I counted the overhead beacons. Twenty! No wonder it was so bright; the light was bouncing and reflecting off the newly waxed floor and shiny tabletops. Light, light, bright light everywhere.

Quickly, I remedied the shining situation with ten blue fluorescent light filters. Now, whenever anyone enters my room, they comment on how calm it feels. They sense calmness but aren't aware it's light filters doing their job. Many students are sensitive to light. These filters are just the trick to calm their nerves. Such a small thing, but left unattended, leads to irritable students (and teachers).

Set up the environment for students. It sounds like a no-brainer, I know. But I've gone into many elementary classrooms that look Pinterest perfect but aren't inviting for students. Adults rave about them, but students crave ownership of their space. Be sure artwork is hung at their eye level, not yours. Be sure to put supplies on shelves they can reach. Have as much as you can available to them. It's *their* classroom. For example, I always have bandaids on a lower shelf in a cabinet so when students need one, they can get it themselves. Not only does autonomy allow students to be responsible, but it permits you more time on task with other students and awards students with a sense of belonging. Research shows that when students experience autonomy, they have a higher success rate. Who doesn't want that?

Give students voice and choice in how the class should be set up. Be sure they are part of the process. When they are part of the process of creating their physical environment, relationships are built and reinforced. They receive a powerful message: I matter. I belong here.

THE POWER OF SMELL

Georgio perfume transports me into my mom's arms. Why? It's her favorite perfume. Whenever I smell it, I associate the scent with my mom. The power of smell and scent is lasting. Aroma arouses emotions and memories. According to research, the number one sense associated with memories is smell (Lewis, 2015). Grapefruit takes me back to my grandma's kitchen table, where she coached me on the fine art of eating grapefruit properly. I see her weathered face and hear her familiar voice and humming as she bustles around the kitchen. Oh, the power of smell. What scent transforms your moment?

When setting up your physical environment, remember to include all five senses. Kids enter my room inhaling stating, "Your room smells good." The other day, a little girl proclaimed, "When I get a house, I want it to smell like this." My room is infused with lavender. I diffuse it all day long. Lavender is touted to be calming, and scent is important. Of course, be mindful of students with allergies and adjust accordingly.

Scents can be calming, but they can also be associated with trauma. I have a friend who lived with abuse and bleach. To this day, she can't stomach the smell of bleach. Scent association is powerful. Let's create positive memories for our students. Scent is one way.

Create an aroma of hospitality. It makes learners feel welcome. They are certain they're welcome when you add welcoming words and actions to aroma. Diffusers with essential oils are a wonderful way to leave lasting positive scent associations. As I said earlier, I use calming lavender. Sometimes I use peppermint and lemon oil during allergy season. The other day, a kindergarten student entered the room and took a whiff and asked, "Why does it smell like candy canes in here?" Students notice the power of smell. Best of all, they'll always remember the sense of belonging and love every time their olfactory glands connect with lavender, peppermint, and lemon. I think it's important to create a cozy, homey feel in your learning environments. Scent is one way to do so. Scents leave lasting impressions, just like the way you treat your students. They will remember you forever because you made them feel like they matter, and you took the time to trademark your scent.

THE POWER OF SOUND

"In a study of elementary students in Manhattan, psychologist Arlene Bronzaft found that children assigned to classrooms on the side of the school facing train tracks were eleven months behind their counterparts on the quieter side of the building. After New York City Transit installed noise abatement equipment on the tracks, a follow-up study found no difference between the groups" (Batterson, 2020).

Sound or the lack of it has a profound effect on students.

Because of a global pandemic, Covid-19, our students didn't return to school in fall 2020 like previous years. School looked different. We operated with virtual and hybrid options. The hybrid students were broken into two groups: A day and B day. Doing this made it possible to adhere to the CDC (Centers for Disease Control and Prevention) guidelines, such as keeping a socially safe distance of six feet apart. To meet the guidelines, we had only eight or eleven students at a time in a class. Immediately, students loved smaller class sizes (obviously, teachers did too). They loved more one-on-one attention, but they loved less noise too. Classes felt calmer without the raucous sounds of 25 or more excited elementary learners. We want talking and collaboration, but apparently, the volume is too distracting for most. To top it off, students asked me to play soft music during student work periods. It's easy to deduce that sound matters to your learners.

Sound can be soothing or energizing. Think about it? Close your eyes right now. What sound calms you? Birds chirping with a bubbling brook? Soft piano music? The sound of rhythmic ocean waves? What energizes you? For me, I love to play soft, soothing music when students enter the room. It sets precedence. I also play calm, instrumental music during writer's workshop. No matter the age of the students, they love it. Research shows that music like Mozart helps students focus (Harvard Health Publishing, 2011). On the other hand, when I want students to move, I play upbeat music with a quick tempo. Music is a wonderful cue for transitions. For example, when you want students to clean up and be at their next place in a certain amount of time, play a song segment. They must be finished by the time the song is over. This expectation works. Music is wonderful for setting the mood, transitions, and learning new material. Everyone remembers what they sing. Sound is a sense to incorporate to reach *all* learners.

I've noticed many students don't seem to have volume control with their voices. We need to model all types of noise levels and teach the volume we expect for different situations. For example, when students are writing, I expect whispers. On the other hand, when creating a team project, they'll be louder using a teamwork voice. These types of voices and volumes need to be modeled and rehearsed. When I had students rehearse whispering, it was shocking to learn that many students couldn't seem to dial back their blasting voice. We live in a noisy world; therefore, we've got to guide our students through this seemingly obvious realm: voice volume control.

When someone walks into your school or classroom, what do they hear? Is it a healthy buzz? Are students using a teamwork voice, or is it silent? There is a time for both, but what is the overall vibe? Is it words of

> "Whatever it takes to help a student focus and concentrate should be *our* focus."

encouragement or condemnation? Is it laughter? Be sure your culture vibrates with uplifting and encouraging sound waves.

THE POWER OF TOUCH

Touch has a huge home in our schools and classrooms. For young students, have a sensory station. The digital days have our young children sensory deprived. Don't believe me? How come they chew their pencils to pieces and knead Play-Doh like it's a precious jewel they've never touched. They crave kneading, rolling, and squeezing the dough. This is just one example of their need to touch. Find ways to incorporate different textures into your lessons. Provide hands-on learning and stations for all ages. Students remember what they touch and do. Benjamin Franklin reinforces this notion, "*Tell me and I forget, teach me and I may remember, involve me and I learn.*"

Try this:

- Put velcro under a table or desk for students to touch. Some students greatly benefit from having a strip of velcro under a table to stroke while they work or listen.
- Let students hold a "fidget." Some students need to hold onto a "fidget" while they listen to a story or directions. As an adult, I constantly roll up my gum wrapper while listening to a conference speaker. So I guess you could say my gum wrapper is a fidget. Whatever it takes to help a student focus and concentrate should be *our* focus.

Think about how the floor feels, the workspaces, the walls, everything. Touch has lasting effects on our students' thinking and learning. Let's be sure to touch our students with healing words and contact, hands-on learning, and sensory moments.

THE POWER OF SIGHT

Recently, I went to the mall with my own kids (not students I call *my* kids). A real brick and mortar mall. Besides enjoying being with family, I felt like a child who had never been out in the world. Sort of like the movie *Elf* when Buddy arrives in New York. When we entered Dillards, I couldn't even count the varied cosmetic counters and lipstick tubes. There were 100s and 100s. My heart raced. My head hurt. Have you ever seen a bobblehead in a car window? I felt like a bobblehead trying to take in all the products reputable cosmetic companies perfectly placed in my path to the shoe department. Oh yeah, I came for shoes. The counters and counters of cosmetic choices swept me away from my original plan, shoes. To make matters worse, I'm a pro at one-click shopping with Amazon where I know what I want, I order with one click, and voila- two days later, it arrives. I exercise my Amazon Prime rights frequently. So, entering a brick and mortar store put me on the brink of needing a straight jacket. Seriously, I was completely overstimulated.

How many of our classrooms, student spaces, and workspaces are like this? Sure, they aren't overstuffed with cosmetics, but how about posters and the latest and greatest cute thing. My visit to the mall got me thinking about how I unintentionally distract students because of too much stuff.

Look at your space from your students' vista point. Is it cluttered? What statement are the decorations conveying? Are they necessary? Were they first introduced to students then hung on the wall to provide scaffolding, or are they dismissed decorations? Be sure everything on the walls has a purpose. What about tabletops? Are they clutter-free, so students have adequate workspace choices? Can you cover up overstuffed shelves with curtains to create serenity?

After asking myself those questions, I made adjustments. Daily before leaving school, I clear all clutter from tabletops to start fresh and new each day. Our classrooms are busy and full of wonderful learning tools. It's easy for stuff to accumulate and get out of hand.

★ **Try This:**

- Intentionally tidy up daily so the "clutter monster" stays somewhat caged.
- View the room from your students' perspective. Sit in their seats (all of them). Is anything blocking a student's view? When I did this, I learned that I always stood in the way of a student's view. They couldn't see what I was showing. When I learned this, I moved. Amazing. The student could then answer all my questions.
- Always think of the room as a workspace for students. How will they work best? If you don't know, ask them.

THE POWER OF TASTE

Since taste is one of our important five senses, I'd be remiss not to include it. For me, taste has to do with cooking in the classroom. Provide frequent opportunities for this. Multiple skills are learned by cooking together, such as reading recipes, expanding vocabulary, following steps in a process, measurement, fractions, and so much more. Relationships are always built around food. Food is a comforting common ground. Purposefully plan lessons tied to tastebuds.

Something special happens when you make and grow your own food. Something special happens when you gather with others to do it. My students made everything from applesauce, butter, ice cream, pancakes, and pizza, to growing and tossing a salad. Students who never ate salad suddenly crunched and munched *their* salad, proclaiming, "I'm a salad person now. *This* salad is good."

Students learn valuable core lessons and understand the value of relationships and community centered around food. Your students will be sure to remember the skills embedded and threaded throughout a class involving food. Tastebuds lend themselves to savoring the lesson.

TAMED BY TIMERS

Do you ever lose yourself in a project? I do. Just yesterday, I had to set the timer so I'd quit writing and get ready for school. Without that annoying beep, beep, I'd kept on writing. In our learning environments, all students benefit from timers. Not only do they provide a visual when you project them like an online countdown timer or online sensory timer, but they also provide the structure we all crave. When projected for all students to see, students begin to learn how to manage their time. I love timers because then I'm not the "bad guy." The timer says it is time to stop, not me. One of my favorite timers for elementary students to use with autonomy is the Miracle Cube Timer, a plastic cube with preset time intervals such as 1, 3, 5, and 10 minutes.

For real, it's called that, and let me tell you—it works like a miracle for students that are having a meltdown and need to go to a calm down area. Meltdown? No problem. Take the Miracle Cube Timer to the calm down area, set it for 5 minutes, and decompress. Voila! Works like a miracle every time. Well, maybe not that amazing, but you get the idea. It works well, putting the student in charge. Self-regulation is a skill we've got to role model and teach.

ENVIRONMENT FLOW

I fell off a ball chair. For real. Our Professional Learning Community (PLC) meetings are held in a comfy space with flexible seating. When I entered the room, the only seat left was a ball chair. I sat on it. Then promptly slid right off the back with my legs up in the air and my bottom on the floor. I was jolted and jarred physically and emotionally embarrassed. Lesson learned: Not all flexible seating is truly flexible and suits everyone.

Flexible seating is just that—flexible. So there is no need to expend time and resources creating a chart. It bothers me to think flexible seating is assigned. What if a learner is assigned a wobble seat for the day, but they don't want to sit on it because they might fall off? Let students sit in whatever seat suits their needs for the day. It's *their* choice.

Give sitting, standing, and no kidding—rolling options. Remember in chapter three the first grader who rolled on the floor? She needed space to roll like a pencil. She'd write a little, roll like a pencil away from the page, then roll back like a pencil and write some more. She took a standardized test in roll-like-a-pencil fashion. Guess what? She had a perfect score. I'm convinced we need to do whatever it takes to set our students up for success, even if it takes creating enough space to roll on the floor like a pencil. Flexible seating is a wonderful way to meet *all* our kids' needs.

Create a caring culture and learning environment with comfortable pillows and multiple seating choices. Provide clipboards and portable tabletops that can move from place to place, allowing for *all* types of learners.

When thinking of your physical environment's flow, be sure to create areas with varied workspaces with varied heights. Set up small, high, round, and low tables, and put desks into table groups serving a dual purpose (individual desk workspace and a table for a group activity). Think of your environment in sections: conducive to collaboration, alone spaces, small group gatherings, and instructional spaces. Physically walk around your learning space and pace the flow as if you were a student. For example, is there plenty of space to line up, or are students running into each other or objects? Are work spaces crowded? Make changes as necessary. Amazingly, something as simple as flow can diminish behavior challenges. The physical set up of furniture is important for successful student flow (and focus).

Lastly, be creative with your learning environment. Once you set up your permanent space, think about other options for places to learn. For example, courtyards outside, the school atrium, a tiny house, an outdoor classroom, etc. Switching up the learning environment exposes your students to options and definitely busts boredom. Be spontaneous. One day, I took students out to our school farm to read to the animals. They loved it. Think outside-the-box, or in this case, think outside-your-classroom. Have fun.

Purposefully plan and create a space and place for *all* types of learners. It sounds like a no-brainer, but how often do we forget to do this? I know I do.

NEXT STEPS:

1. What are some physical environment needs you can meet that you aren't currently meeting? How will you meet them? Who can help you?
2. How will you set up your classroom/school flow to meet the needs of *all* learners?
3. Ask your students about their comfort in your classroom/school. Their answers will guide you.
4. No matter your students' ages, what are some ways you can incorporate the five senses into your lessons or throughout your day?

CONNECT:

Connect with other warrior teachers and share what you do on Twitter or Instagram. **Share what you do in your classroom to help students learn by using the five senses. What were the results?** Your stories and pictures may be just what someone needs for encouragement to be a warrior for their students. You make a difference. Let's create a community, a movement amplifying *all* students. Use the hashtag #BeTheirWarrior.

5

CREATE A CULTURE CONDUCIVE TO ALL EMOTIONAL NEEDS

Create a positive culture that ensures and embodies the emotional needs of *all* learners.

> *"Students who are loved at home come to school to learn, and students who aren't, come to school to be loved."*

*J*n his quote, Nicholas Ferroni expresses exactly why attending to Maslow's Hierarchy of basic needs is important. Students aren't ready to learn until their basic needs, such as feeling safe, belonging, and love, are met.

One way to ensure everyone feels loved and has a sense of belonging is to create a classroom family vibe. The other day, a student shared, "I love what you said—that we're like a classroom family." Having a sense of family nurtures relationships and cultivates a positive, caring culture.

CREATE A FAMILY-LIKE CULTURE

Creating a family-like culture is not only a good idea, but it's backed by studies that conclude social connection leads to achievement.

> *"Studies on thousands of students show that learners who are better socially connected to their teachers and classmates are significantly more engaged and achieve better than their less well-connected peers,"* notes Hunter Gehlbach, an associate professor of education. *"When we allow ourselves to be vulnerable, acknowledge our imperfections, and tell our stories, we show our students that we are, in fact, more like them than they may imagine"* (Pandolpho, 2018).

In my class, we're a classroom family. We treat each other the way we want to be treated. When problems arise daily in every family (classroom/school), we pause and work out challenges through a family meeting. It's an excellent way for everyone to be heard. This is "voice and choice" as a life skill. Everyone shares ideas to solve the problem. I write it on a chart. Then, collectively we decide which solution best meets our needs.

Kids rise to what is expected of them. Together, they work through projects, challenges, and victories. Together, we celebrate. Together, they create their norms and expectations, and together we hold each other accountable.

The key to making all this work and stick like velcro is consistency. It's essential to praise with appropriate responses set by the class regularly. When you do, students begin to compliment, congratulate and honor each other. They kindly inform peers to follow expectations. Because everyone wants to contribute and belong, a classroom family culture helps every single student feel valued.

Families share. Students love to share their own family stories and their daily lives with each other. They learn about each other's interests through morning meetings, but I also ensure they have time to share every Friday. We call it sharing time; it is like "Show & Tell." An article in *Edutopia* touted the importance of sharing time for all ages. Even high school seniors need "show and tell" (Alber, 2017). Show and tell is a beautiful way to develop oral language and social skills. Even the edgiest and most challenging students sit still and participate during this time because everyone has the spotlight and chance to shine.

Respect is role modeled and expected. I've noticed that I have to explain to students what respectful behavior looks like and sounds like. I have to tell them that rolling your eyes is disrespectful. It has become such a habit for some, they think it's acceptable. A classroom family teaches and role models respect and apologizes when disrespectful.

Often kids don't know what they need to say to others because kindness and resolve aren't used in their own families. So I role model how to treat others and provide a language framework. It's important to share feelings. Teaching students "I statements" when they have disagreements gives them a language framework.

The frame goes like this:

When you...

I feel...

Can you please...

When there's a conflict, teach learners to listen to each other. Lead them to reside on a resolution. Communication skills are life skills serving students well beyond the classroom. My students truly don't tattle (much–they are six) because I don't work out their problems for them. I've taught them how to talk to each other and solve their problems. I've found it doesn't matter if it's a six-year-old or a teenager; they still need a framework for communicating conflict. A conflict resolution framework gives them the language required to restore the relationship.

Constantly monitor students' body language and emotions. Get to know what their nonverbal cues lead to. Adjust what you are doing if necessary and assist them as needed. Meet their emotional needs consistently.

You are the light for your students. When they've received a negative comment, they need eleven positive comments to counteract it. Intentionally focus and look for the good. Give specific, positive feedback enabling students to repeat what they do well and believe in themselves. When you do, you're meeting their basic needs of love and acceptance, allowing them to be more ready to learn.

Creating a classroom family culture teaches essential life skills. Laugh together, cry together, and ride every wave of emotion together; you're a classroom family.

VOICE & CHOICE

Voice and choice have been around since the first baby took its first breath. With every scream and wail, a baby communicates to its responding parents. Their needs must be met. They've learned early how to exercise their right to voice and choice. The parents bustle about giving the choices to calm the voice. Of course, it doesn't work like that in our learning environments, but we've got to listen to *all* students' pleas. (Even if they are speaking through inappropriate behavior, they have a need that requires being emotionally met.) To meet all learners' emotional needs, we've got to be mindful of creating a culture that encourages students' voices and giving choices that empower and meet our learners' needs.

Voice and choice are more than a slogan. It's being intentional about listening to your students and designing your plans and environment around their input.

Students' input kindles engagement and creates a culture where their ideas are valued. Listening to students' needs, wants, and desires gives them a reason to return to your room. It creates a culture sending the message: You matter. You are important. You are heard. You are seen. You are special and contribute to what we do here. Voice and choice need to be woven into all fibers of your culture: whether it is expressing how to solve problems, determining rewards and consequences, sharing preferences for the physical environment, or steering their learning direction. Students' input is valuable.

Students' interests lead to learning. For example, at the beginning of each year, we have a chart titled: *My Hopes and Dreams For First Grade*. Students and families add Post-it notes to the chart sharing what they want to learn and gain from the first grade. I make it happen. At the end of the year, we revisit the chart and discuss how each hope and dream came true. Any grade level or leader can use a *My Hopes and Dreams* chart. I even use it with each grade level I teach as a STEM teacher.

Teaching your students' interests ignites the love of learning. The following is an example of teaching to their interests.

My students wanted to learn about bees. Their desire launched our project-based- learning (PBL) project: "What's All The Buzz About Bees?" We created a K.W.L.(Know. Want to Know. Learn.) chart to find out what they already knew about bees and discover what the students wanted to learn. Students read books and researched about bees. We invited an expert from the Tidewater Beekeepers Association to bring an observation hive to our school. He taught the importance of bees and pollination. After learning more about bees, my students became advocates. They created a mantra: "Save the bees! No bees, no food!" Feeding their interest, we brainstormed ways to save bees. Also, we took a field trip to a real bee yard. The students donned beekeeper suits and conducted a hive inspection. Our bee expert taught students the importance of being a beekeeper. He taught them that beekeepers maintain the bee population to pollinate our food crops. Then came the journey of building a beehive, creating flyers and posters about the importance of bees and beekeeping, writing books about bee facts, creating t-shirts with their slogan, "Save the Bees," and advocating in the school and community. Students gave out bee-friendly flower seed packages with their slogan and flyers to people in the community. The project culminated with a school-wide exhibition and presentation of the hive to a nearby high school farm manager.

This PBL project incorporated learning standards from every academic area and deeper learning, such as critical thinking and problem-solving. Students used collaboration, creativity, and communication, thereby keeping engaged. Students took a topic they were interested in and transferred their learning into being good citizens. Listening and acting on what they said they wanted to learn paid huge dividends.

Voice, choice, and autonomy cultivate motivation. Motivation, coupled with a loving, caring environment, immensely engages students—achievement sky-rockets.

Creating voice and choice takes intentionally listening to your students and designing your plans and environment around their input. Too often, we silence our students to meet the demands and standards that

> "Voice and choice are more than a slogan. It's being intentional about listening to your students and designing your plans and environment around their input."

must be taught. When, in fact, we can tailor our students' interests around the same standards leading to engagement and gains in student achievement. Let's hear from our students and give them the choices they need to learn. Be their warrior, allow voice and choice.

MISTAKES ARE FOR LEARNING

Oscar Wilde said, "*Experience is simply the name we give our mistakes.*"

I love that quote. True experience is learning to do better and move forward from mistakes. An aged adage sums it up: The definition of insanity is repeating the same thing expecting different results.

Therefore, true experience is reflecting and learning from mistakes to move forward. Moving forward involves changing what didn't work.

Using the story of Leo the Late Bloomer as a model, my students know learning is a process. We all develop in our own time. Students work collaboratively giving kind, specific, and helpful feedback, which helps them improve. Students set goals and record their progress. Progress is celebrated. When students make progress, the class applauds their effort, propelling them to learn more. Do more. It's positive peer pressure. We treat everyone with equal care and respect. Still, equity education is provided, so each child gets what they need emotionally and academically to develop and master standards. Progress over perfection is savored. Students learn to fail forward and keep developing.

I am a role-model making mistakes and refining my own work. So students don't complain about refining their work. Some days, I make mistakes without even trying, and my students gently remind me that "mistakes are for learning." If we continue to make mistakes but don't grow from them, then we're not learning. It's the same for our students too. When they make mistakes, we've got to provide precise feedback (one of my colleagues calls it "feed-it-forward") for our students to learn and grow.

Additionally, emphasize the importance of students doing their very best and not comparing them to others. Their best isn't someone else's best. My best looks different from their best too. The goal is to progress. Strive to do your best. Period.

My friend Helen Stanphil, an author of young adult novels, died from a brain tumor but left a legacy through writing. She shared with my students how to grow as writers. She told them writing was similar to rebounding in basketball. How many times is the first shot missed, but rebounds save the day? Lots! What wonderful advice. I think we all need to remember to rebound in all areas of our life because mistakes are for learning. Learn from them, and rebound. Lots!

Carol Dweck's growth mindset is valid and popular. You can incorporate growth mindset lessons into your morning meetings. Also, I love to teach lessons through literature, such as through the picture book *Bubblegum Brain*. (I've found older kids still like picture books too.) Growth mindset stories help kids realize our learning is a lifelong journey, and it's truly okay to make mistakes as long as we grow and make progress.

"Mistakes are for learning" is a mantra for me; it's a motto in our classroom family. When you create a safe learning environment, your learners take risks. They'll be brave. They won't be afraid to fail. The word fail is summed up as follows:

First
Attempt
In
Learning

I stole that acronym from somewhere along my educational journey, but it's true. Failure isn't final. To fail is just a first attempt in learning. When you create a culture of failing forward, your learners will seek assistance and try, try again.

12 ENCOURAGING PHRASES TO BUILD RESILIENCE IN KIDS

1. I love the way you always try so hard.
2. Keep going, you're nearly there.
3. I'm so proud of how you always give things your best try.
4. I know this is hard but I also know you will get there in the end.
5. What other ways could you approach this?
6. Is there a way I can help you without doing the task for you?
7. I believe in you. You've got this.

8. Just take a few deep breaths and try again/another way.

9. Believing in yourself takes lots of practice.

10. Sometimes we have to fail and then try again, and maybe even fail and try again in order to succeed.

11. You've done it once, I know you can do it again.

12. You are very brave. (Educate2Empower, n.d.)

THE ATTITUDE IN WHICH A LESSON IS TAUGHT SPEAKS LOUDER THAN AN ELABORATE PLAN

Culture begins with attitude. Believe in every student. This belief sets the tone and foundation for relationships and student success. Be excited. Be understanding and help students through their challenges. Be loving and willing to change if a lesson isn't going how you thought it would. Each year, we have a different mix of students that remind me of varied fabric textures and patterns like squares on a quilt. They are all woven together to make up our class, but they are all so uniquely different. The greatest thing that we can do for them is to adapt and meet their emotional needs. Just because a lesson was fantastic one year doesn't mean it will be this year with *this* group of students. However, there is one constant: our positive attitude. Our enthusiasm and positive attitude will always be contagious and allow all students to soar. Our belief in them will always be in style. They will remember our positive attitude and expectations more than the lesson plan framework.

Having a positive, loving, enthusiastic attitude—one that lights up and says, "Oh, there you are. I'm so glad you are here"—is vital in establishing a caring culture. No matter students' backgrounds or abilities, they want to be with you, and please you because they know you care and you will help them. Your positive attitude permeates throughout your class and school, causing students to grow and learn. It's contagious and more powerful than a perfectly planned lesson.

Educator Danny Steele outlines another attitude that's extremely important for meeting all students' emotional needs: "*I think teachers are at their best not when delivering a brilliantly innovative lesson, but when they are demonstrating patience and compassion toward a student who struggles.*"

Students will always remember how we make them feel more than all the bells and whistles in an engaging lesson. Therefore, we need to put on garments of enthusiasm, patience, praise, and compassion every day.

Sometimes I lose my patience with students. When I do, I immediately regret it. Therefore, it's what you do after you lose your patience that matters. I sincerely apologize. I take a few moments to breathe slowly in and out...in and out. I reset. I improve. I love. Ultimately, I role model humanness. My students get to see how I handle losing my patience in a healthy, constructive way. They witness relationships restored. We can't be superhuman 100% of the time. (Wouldn't that be nice!) So, in those moments, my attitude matters more than any innovative lesson. It becomes a teachable moment of how to handle emotions and mistakes in a healthy, restorative way.

TAKE A MENTAL TIMEOUT

My husband's eyes locked with mine. We sat around our dining room table, stunned, searching for the cause. "I-I-I-I am a g-g-g-g-ood b-b-b-boy," our son stated repeatedly. When did this stuttering start? Why did he feel the need to repeat *these* words? Of course, he was a good boy. We bestowed love upon him every day of his life. We also disciplined him. Another form of love. His anxiety was so thick it settled over our dinner table like a cumulonimbus. Our fun-loving, smiley boy had a storm cloud hanging over his head.

After days of soul searching, my mommy gut instinct uncovered the mystery. His kindergarten teacher was a yeller. Our son's teacher spent a large portion of the day raising his voice and yelling. Although our son wasn't the brunt of the slicing words, he felt the stress and pain. He anxiously wondered when the yelling words of disapproval would wind his way. The teacher we hand-picked and touted to be the best was stressing our son out. So, we moved our son out. Sometimes the best teacher can be the wrong fit.

After one day in a new kindergarten room, the cloud went away. His smile returned. The stuttering stopped. Miraculous? No. The power of emotions. *All* kids feel our emotions, whether we intend for them to or not.

Our students feel what we feel. We need to constantly reflect on our behavior and actions to ensure they aren't negatively impacting our students. Sure, there may be a day or two that we raise our voices or get frustrated. But this shouldn't ever be our modus operandi. Yelling isn't effective. Yelling isn't acceptable. Calm, loving voices always win no matter how challenging the behavior. Speak life with your words and tone of voice. When we are feeling stressed, or the kids are going crazy, stop. Take a mental timeout. Breathe. Remember to respond with love and kindness. Sometimes, we need to take a quick mental break to respond with emotions that meet our students' emotional needs.

Kids don't come to school with the motive to make it a difficult day for the teacher or to not do their best. Our job is to take them from where they are to where they can go through support, resources, encouragement, and a caring, positive culture

★ Try This for Challenging Students

Beyond a doubt, we want all students to succeed, but what do we do when they have a meltdown or need some time away from an activity that may trigger a negative behavior response? I've found that a calm down basket filled with various sensory items works well. I role model how it is supposed to be used. The items may look like toys, but they truly work for most elementary children. I also role model how to set a timer for a student's amount of time to stay at the calm down basket. The calm down basket is like rebooting a computer. It gives the student a moment to step away from a stressful situation, relax, and gather composure. When they return to the activity, usually after 5 minutes, they engage without conflict. They are still expected to follow all directions and complete all academic requirements. Sometimes, they just need a break to diffuse and begin fresh to do what is expected.

Being a warrior for students is finding ways for them to access all lessons, so they have success. For me, I don't care if a student sits, rolls, stands, or needs a calm down basket as long as they are kind, caring, respectful, and complete the task. Meeting their needs with support helps them experience success. Success breeds success.

What if we embrace challenging kids instead of thinking: if only they'd do...(insert your own words here.) Reframe your thinking. Think: *What happened to you*? Instead of *What's wrong with you*? I know it's tough. There were days as I pulled into the school parking lot that my stomach was so twisted with anxiety that I could hardly stand. I never knew what roadblock I'd face from multiple challenging students on any given day. I was emotionally spent from meeting their needs, teaching content, and anticipating triggers and meltdowns. Many times it was difficult to focus on students' needs because of so many disruptions. Some days I felt like I was running a circus rather than teaching.

But the greatest challenges bring the greatest rewards. Victories were evident in changed lives, students and mine. The daily disturbances led to a greater appreciation for those that have challenges and allowed me to grow and become a better educator despite the obstacles; it gave me deeper empathy for those who struggle. I'm so thankful I never gave up because rewards followed the temporary affliction.

WHAT DO YOU DO WITH AN ANGRY STUDENT?

Anger is energy. Therefore, it needs to be expended. When students are angry, take the opportunity to teach them positive ways to expend their angry energy. For example: take a walk, use items in a calm down basket.

A student came back to school after being away for almost one year because of school closures caused by the global pandemic 2020. When he returned to school, he got angered quickly when he didn't finish projects or they didn't work out like he'd imagined. The new pace from home life to school life had him flustered. When he got super angry, I explained to him that anger was okay. I told him everyone gets angry, but how you react to your anger is key. You need to diffuse your angry energy in a safe, healthy way. I gave him two options: 1. Take a walk 2. The calm down basket. (I offered only two options from the calm down basket. 1 item was something to squeeze like a stress ball. The other item was a rubber stretchy sensory item he could pull. He selected the rubber stretchy item to pull.) It truly worked. In a matter of minutes, he was able to re-engage in learning and join the class.

Remember, anger is energy that must be spent. It's up to you to lead learners to healthy, appropriate ways to expend anger. Suggestion: expand their vocabulary for the word *anger* by modeling using words like "annoyed, tense, frustrated. "

CALM DOWN BASKET IDEAS

- Flexible ball (Breath in when you pull it out. Exhale when you push it in.)
- Sensory rubber toys to squeeze, pull, and stretch
- 12- 3 oz. paper cups to stack
- A book about feelings or anger

- Mini bubbles
- Playdough
- Net tube with a marble in it
- Glitter jar or wand
- Bouncy ball
- Straws
- Pipe Cleaners
- Pinwheel
- Anti-Stress rollerball
- Jumping frogs
- Liquid motion bubble timer- Sensory

CREATE A CALM DOWN SPACE

Students who get overwhelmed need a space to be quiet or reset before their behavior spirals downhill. They need a place to go when they can't identify why they are feeling frustrated or angry. They need a safe space. Create a safe space to calm down.

Be sure to model how to use the space and the calm down basket. Set specific expectations for the space. I model how to set a timer when a student enters the space so all students know that they have a time limit. The time can be reset, but the expectation is always to re-engage.

Sometimes educators think that students will use the calm down space or the calm down basket as a way to get out of work. Truly, this doesn't happen when you create the expectations and consistently reinforce them. Also, I let all students touch the sensory items in the calm down basket when I introduce it. For those that don't need it, the novelty wears off. For those that need it, it's a wonderful tool that works.

SPOTLIGHT STUDENTS REPEATEDLY & ROUTINELY

Being in the spotlight bolsters self-esteem, produces positive character, and encourages students to grow and be their best. When students see what others are doing well, they want to rise to that standard too. When students feel safe, they want to share. When they share, they feel important. When they feel important, they contribute. When they contribute, their energy is focused on being beneficial instead of attention-seeking, burdensome behavior. They feel like their input and work matters, which are basic needs to flourish. Create an emotionally safe culture.

Putting students in the spotlight is core to a positive, caring culture. It can be challenging to do some days with 30 or more students, especially if you are a resource teacher, but being intentional about it is the first step to ensuring every student gets in the limelight every day. Come up with a plan that fits your style and situation. I'm usually intentional about having a certain table for each day share out. I use call sticks. (More on this in chapter 7.) Ensure everyone shares their work with each other every day, so they all have a spotlight moment.

 Try This

- Turn and Talk Strategy- Have students who don't feel comfortable sharing with the whole group, turn and talk with a partner. This is a way they can successfully share, communicate, and process their thoughts. Be sure to model "Turn and Talk" expectations, eliciting a safe environment to share.
- Draw your ideas. Students who don't feel comfortable sharing with the whole group orally can draw their thoughts on a whiteboard, iPad, or piece of paper and hold it up.
- Build trust by letting students share with only you first. I've found that when trust is built over time, even the shyest students want to communicate orally with the whole group.

Be sure spotlighting students is part of your culture and daily dynamics. The following examples are routinely and intentionally planned spotlight moments: Author's chair, snack basket, sharing time like "show and tell," turn and talk, sharing work through Booksnaps, Flipgrid, blogs, podcasts, or anything really. The list goes on. (Insert here what you do to help students be in the spotlight daily.)

Empower them! Give them the driver's seat. Teach students to coach other students. Lead them to teach lessons and read aloud. Everyone wants their moment to shine. They'll petition to be the one to read aloud for the day. They'll beg to teach a lesson. A byproduct of their drive to be in the spotlight is they'll practice and learn skills without being told to do it. They'll take ownership of their learning.

Putting learners in the spotlight repeatedly and routinely creates intrinsic motivation. In return, they are engaged, happy to contribute, and genuinely desire to learn. Their desire, even love of learning, leads to higher achievement. Being in the spotlight regularly cultivates positive character traits, self-esteem, and personal growth.

APPRECIATION AFFIRMATION

When you see work or behaviors you are cultivating, stop and highlight them. Let students shine. When you do this frequently, it usually results in others saying, "Good job so and so for...." Students affirm peers in the way you've role modeled. Always state the specific behavior or task. Be specific. Specific can be duplicated. For example, "Good job writing a complete sentence with an adjective." When you tell a student, "Good job," they need to know what was good and why so that they can do it again. Learners praise others and complete tasks because of the intrinsic reward of doing a good job, their best.

Just like taking a bath isn't permanent, neither are words of affirmation. Apply words of encouragement and affirmation often and see your learners shine.

"To reach a child's mind, a teacher must capture his heart. Only if a child feels right can he think right."

— HAIM G. GINOTT

Our learners' emotional needs are supreme. Without meeting them, no significant learning takes place. See chapter 2 for ideas on assessing emotional needs. We cultivate a positive, caring culture by setting the tone with relational routines, listening, and ensuring everyone contributes and feels valued. Students need to feel safe and supported. Deep-seated emotional needs are met when you build relationships and love *all* learners.

NEXT STEPS:

1. What are some emotional needs you can meet that you aren't currently meeting? How will you meet them? Who can help you?
2. Ask your students about their feelings regularly.
3. How will you role model and guide students when helping them regulate their emotions?
4. No matter your students' ages, what are some ways you can incorporate Social Emotional Learning into your lesson or throughout your day?
5. How will you be intentional about ensuring every student has the spotlight daily for a moment?

CONNECT:

Connect with other warrior teachers and share what you do on Twitter or Instagram. Share how you spotlight students. Share what you do for a calm down space. **Share how you develop resilient kids. Share how you incorporate SEL. What were the results?** Your stories and pictures may be just what someone needs for encouragement. You make a difference. Let's create a community, a movement amplifying *all* students. Use the hashtag #BeTheirWarrior.

6

FOSTER A CULTURE FOR ALL LEARNING NEEDS

Fabricate a culture that embraces, engages, and facilitates growth for *all* learners.

SLEEP, CREEP, AND LEAP

My dad is a gardener. He's not just *any* gardener. He's a skilled gardener with a passion for plants. He doesn't have a green thumb; he has two. I grew up with the DaVinci of gardening. He taught me a valuable lesson when we were planting trees and bushes. He taught me that the first year you plant a tree or bush, it appears to be sleeping because you can't see visible growth. The plant is putting down roots. It's putting all energy into establishing roots to hold it in the ground and provide nutrients. Roots are vital. They're the lifeline—the foundation.

During the second year, the plant displays minimal growth. It creeps because it's still adjusting to the environment and deepening its roots. Growth is still happening, but mostly underground. By the third year, the plant flourishes. It appears to leap in growth because all the growth is on the outside. It's visible. However, if it hadn't taken two years to establish a good root system, it wouldn't have been able to leap and show significant visible growth.

Sleep, creep, and leap is a gardening parallel for learners' growth. When we first learn, it takes a lot of practice and repetition. It is sinking into our brain fibers. We're digesting newly learned information. Our students may appear to be sleeping when, in reality, they are processing and digesting newly learned information. The learning, growing, and changing is happening on the inside (in their brains). It takes time to see the fruit of their learning displayed on the outside. So don't give up when you don't physically see growth. Keep nurturing. They need more time and experience when it looks like they're asleep.

With more time and experiences tied to the same content, they'll display some level of learning or competency. They'll creep along. In time with repeated, hands-on, life-applicable lessons, they'll leap. They'll blossom with knowledge. It appears to happen in a day when, in reality, it takes years of building a foundation of background knowledge and experiences. It takes years of love and meeting basic needs before significant learning takes place. Remember, our students *are* learning. They're always learning, just at different rates. Some sleep, creep and leap. No matter what stage your learners are currently in, do whatever it takes to continue their learning journey and provide experiences for learning success. It takes time. It takes repetition tied to relevance. It takes nurturing and patience.

CAPITALIZE, ILLUMINATE, AND SHARE GIFTS & TALENTS

There is a theory in organizational development called *appreciative inquiry* that I subscribe to as an educator and parent. Instead of exclusively focusing on what's wrong and trying to fix it, identify what's right and replicate it (Batterson, 2020).

Create a culture of acceptance and growth capitalizing on gifts and talents. One example is as simple as having students that are really good at writing work with students who aren't as good at writing. While sharing their gift, they help others improve. I have some students who are really good at ST-Math, a visual instructional program that builds a deep conceptual understanding of math through rigorous learning and creative problem-solving. They coach other students through their learning hurdles. This becomes such an integral part of our culture that students automatically help others and applaud each other's progress. It's beautiful.

An excellent example of students sharing gifts and talents is through a mentoring program. No matter what age you lead, I highly suggest setting up some sort of peer mentorship. Here's why: Fifth-grade students came to my class daily to assist struggling readers. This was a win-win relationship. My first graders read with someone keeping them engaged and learning; the fifth-graders became strong mentors and role models. One fifth-grader, known as a "trouble maker," excelled with my first graders. He was never a problem when working with them. In fact, when I saw him in the hallway, he walked a bit taller, smiled, and said, "Hi, Mrs. Hall!" It's wonderful to know that this mentorship program helped him to be a better person. Peer mentoring is a symbiotic relationship allowing students to share their gifts and talents and shine while helping others learn.

Another example of illuminating gifts and talents is capitalizing on students' strengths. William was an extremely active child with a smile literally stretching a mile across his face like the Cheshire Cat. His skin rippled waves of abundant energy, usually resulting in some classroom catastrophe like broken chairs or broken shelves. William tripped over his own feet because he moved so rapidly. Forget about sitting in a chair; he couldn't hold still. He was the epitome of the main character in the book *No, David* by David Shannon. He loved to talk, and his mile-wide smile lit up any space. Capitalizing on this strength, I gave him a job to greet people and hold up a sign at our project-based-learning exhibition. None of these tasks required him to concentrate or hold still. His sole task was to greet, welcome, and recruit guests to visit the library to see a video we created. He was wonderful at it—the best. Do you know what happened? When we reflected, and students shared their celebrations, William raised his hand. He enthusiastically shared, "I's excited about our Expo. I love mine's job!" William experienced success. As we know, success breeds success.

Throughout the year, William used to say, "I was bad. Now I is good. I love our class." (Apparently, before landing in our class, he had been in trouble daily.) It's disturbing that before the age of six, he perceived himself as a bad person. We're our students' inner voice. What we say to them and how we treat them becomes the voice in their head, and then ultimately, it has the power to come true. Choose words and actions wisely.

William came to our class, not knowing any letters and letter sounds. At the end of the year, he read everything on the walls as we walked down the hallway. He processed everything out loud in a very raucous voice. He was disruptive and had a monumental challenge focusing his attention. Still, he learned because I found a way to capitalize on his strengths. Students shine and feel empowered when we put them in positions to use their strengths. Create a culture capitalizing on students' gifts and talents, bringing out the best in every student. Feed their strengths and be their warrior.

BE MINDFUL OF CULTURAL NEEDS & EMBRACE DIVERSITY

Cultivate a culture that embraces diversity and acknowledges different cultures learn and do things differently. For example, some students do not make direct eye contact with the teacher. In Western culture, this may signify that the person is not paying attention to the speaker. However, in many cultures, making direct eye contact with the teacher (or any other person of authority) is a sign of disrespect. Their families teach many students not to make eye contact (Alrubail, 2016).

So be mindful of different cultures and respect their way of learning. If you don't know, ask. Find out and meet their learning needs.

I'm not a diversity expert, but I *am* all about reaching *all* kids. This tiny section needs to be a whole library. However, I feel this entire book lends itself to recognizing and embracing each student's needs. This book is geared toward equity and celebrating diversity. It's geared to support, amplify, and reach *all* students regardless of background and ability.

So why did I include a sliver section like this for such an important topic? I wanted us to remember cultural differences such as eye contact mentioned above and any other similar gestures that we think others should do based on our foundational experiences.

Teach students to learn and listen to each other. We are stronger through our differences. Teach students how to agree to disagree.

> "Let differences reinforce relationships instead of divide."

Everyone's perspective is valuable. Let differences reinforce relationships instead of divide.

ATTEND TO ATTENTION

"The average human attention span is now shorter than a goldfish's—seriously. A study found that the average human attention span fell from 12 seconds in 2000 (or around the time smartphones hit the scene) to 8 seconds in 2018. In comparison, scientists believe goldfish have an attention span of 9 seconds (Web, 2018). We're bombarded digitally, and our brains get hooked on fast-paced stimuli. As a result, it's difficult to pay attention to any one thing for very long. Conversely, it makes it hard to hold anyone's attention for more than a few minutes. This creates a challenge for educators.

Multiple studies state most adults can attend up to 20 minutes in a traditional learning environment. (Not screen-based. The previous statistic is screen time attention span.) Hence the reason TED Talks are 18 minutes. The younger the learner, the lesser their attention span. For example, I was always told learners can focus on direct instruction for as many minutes as they are old. If this is true, a six-year-old can attend for six minutes. Wow! We may cognitively know this to be accurate, but how many of us design our lessons with our students' attention spans in mind?

Shorter attention spans are no surprise to educators. I know I've heard multiple educators lament that students' attention spans are shorter with the rise of digital days.

We may not like this reality. (I know I don't.) But to meet *all* our learners' needs, we've got to change with the tides and think of ways to keep them all engaged, despite their diminishing attention spans. An important message is that learners better function with short stints of direct instruction. So it's now our job of cutting through short attention spans to meaningfully engage *all* learners.

 Try This

- Implement the 10 - 2 rule. For every 10 minutes of information shared, give learners 2 minutes to digest new information through journaling, thinking, or using the "Turn & Talk" strategy.
- Allow for body movement after 10 minutes. A quick brain break of 10 jumping jacks is all it takes for younger children. Set a timer for older students and allow them to get up and move. They return when the timer goes off.
- Plan hands-on, life-applicable lessons.
- Plan engaging learning stations.
- Incorporate technology as a learning tool.
- Use an Instructional Framework for planning and teaching. My school district utilizes the following Instructional Framework for Planning: 5%= Learning Outcomes/Essential Question, 20%= Direct Instruction (I do), 65%= Student Work Period (We do, You do independently), 10%= Debrief (Collaboratively reflect on learning, assess learning to guide instruction).
- Structure your lessons with this essential concept in mind: The *first* thing you say is *most* remembered. The *last* thing you say is the *second most* remembered.

ENGAGEMENT ISN'T AN OPTION

Engagement begins with a positive, caring culture. Then it continues by designing interesting lessons that lead to a love of learning. Creating hands-on, life-applicable experiences for students is essential. Remember, though; they never take the place of love, care, and security. Always meet students' basic needs first, and learning will take place.

Life isn't a worksheet. Hands-on applicable learning sticks; therefore, it's far-reaching to teach skills in context. For example, teach grammar and punctuation skills through writing. Don't inundate students with grammar worksheets. Instead, expose them to rich literature, providing a model of correct grammar. Model using proper grammar and punctuation, and then model editing using an editor's checklist. Students learn correct punctuation and grammar through writing better than drill sheets because writing is a life skill. Students learn to measure capacity by cooking and using measuring cups and measuring spoons. So, the next time you look at a worksheet, ask yourself the following questions: How can I make this life-applicable? How can I make this hands-on? How can I make this into a game? How can I involve *all* students? Fun, life-applicable lessons are automatically engaging.

 "Creativity Takes Courage"

— HENRY MATISSE

After reading Hope and Wade King's book *The Wild Card* (2018), I was inspired to do a room transformation based on my students' interests. Wanting to do a transformation was a pretty amazing feat since I read the book in the springtime, and my energy level lent itself to uninspired lessons. However, their words and examples in the book rekindled my love for creating and teaching exciting lessons.

With newfound inspiration, I tapped into my students' interests causing me to transform our classroom into the popular Minecraft game and correlate it with math. Students dressed up in Minecraft glasses, used pick ax pencils, and created a base out of Lego blocks. Then, in teams, students measured the perimeter. They worked in teams to engineer a creeper trap (Creepers are the bad guys in the game). Students loved it when I dressed up like a creeper! We even sang the theme song changing the lyrics to measurement vocabulary. Every single student was engaged. When lessons are centered around the students' interests, hands-on, and differentiated, behavior problems are few because everyone is engaged in learning.

Consider doing a classroom transformation. One year I thought: I can't do it with *this* class. However, I decided to take my own advice and be brave. Squashing my excuse of *the current class was too wild and challenging,* I did SCOOPS Ice Cream Shop. It *was* totally wild. There was ice everywhere. The room volume was louder than devoted fans at an intense football game, but they learned. They read fiction and non-fiction stories about ice cream. They learned to retell a story, write similes, write stories, steps in a process, read and follow a recipe, measure, and many scientific principles and math standards. Best of all, they made their own ice cream and ate it. It was messy and wild. But the moments are etched in their memories forever. Experiences like this tied to emotions and senses light a fire to learn.

Big, engaging lessons like room transformations and making ice cream are fun and appealing. However, it's the day-to-day consistency and engagement that reap dividends. You create engagement by setting up math, literacy, science, and free exploration STEM stations. The stations are multi-level and self-checking. Every day make sure lessons are hands-on, relevant, and multi-level where kids differentiate their learning. Ongoing formative and summative assessment allows for targeted teaching and high student achievement. You don't have to do room transformations for kids to be engaged. Although, they are super fun and memorable.

To keep students interested, incorporate an element of surprise. For example, one day, I had a box of Lucky Charms cereal sitting out. The students saw it, and it created a buzz. I heard them say, "I wonder what we are going to do with those today?" We used it for sorting, adding, subtracting, and graphing. Engagement doesn't always have to "WOW" the kids. With precision planning and a caring culture, it happens daily.

Have fun, and your students will have fun. Purposefully plan a fun experience tied to standards and students' interests. This type of lesson requires more creativity and planning. Still, it keeps you fresh and creative because you're thinking of your students' interests and how to bring learning alive for them. Tap into your personal strengths and interests, align them with your standards, and bring learning alive. For example, I love nature and music, and kids enjoy learning through cooking. Therefore, I bring gardening, music, and cooking into the classroom. Connect kids to agriculture. Kids who don't excel in other areas excel during these types of experiences. It sparks a love of learning. I have a student who struggles with reading but totally excels at the scientific process and inquiry. Another student who struggles with academics became a beekeeper. Students are engaged and achieve when you plan lessons around their interests.

If I were reading this, this would be the place I might put the book down and say, "That's all nice, but I don't have that kind of time." Please let me reassure you, like you, I have multiple mandates, time restraints, and assessments required of me. They sap my energy and drain my desire to do extra. They don't even (in my opinion) lead to engagement. So that's why I cling to my passion for making learning fun, relevant, hands-on, and new. Fun lessons keep *me* going. When I'm having fun, the students are sure to have fun too.

You are educators who make a difference by meeting *all* learning needs. It's easier to do when you're having fun. So intentionally find time to incorporate engaging lessons. Start small. How do you eat an elephant? One bite at a time. Take a bite. When you experience success, it will lead you to take another bite. The students' excitement and engagement will lead you to take another and another. Just do something more today than you did yesterday. And leave kids wondering and wanting more. Give them a reason to come to school the next day.

Student engagement thrives by building a positive culture, teaching to students' interests, scaffolding students through challenges, and explicit expectations. Listen to your kids' interests and marry standards to

> "Intentionally find time to incorporate engaging lessons. Start small.
> How do you eat an elephant? One bite at a time. Take a bite."

them. Use your hobbies and strengths to create engaging lessons. These lesson moments last a life-time because students are emotionally invested, have fun, and learn. High engagement leads to high achievement.

By building relationships and a positive, caring culture, students are happily engaged; it isn't an option. All the rest is the icing on the cake.

DIFFERENTIATED EXPERIENCES ENGAGE *ALL* LEARNERS

Provide differentiated instruction, not different instruction. "Differentiated instruction in academically diverse classrooms seeks to provide appropriately challenging learning experiences for *all* their students. Teachers realize that sometimes a task that lacks challenge for some learners is frustratingly complex to others" (ASCD, 2021).

Differentiated instruction aims for the same learning results and standards with high expectations. It's differentiated because it is tailored to the learner's unique needs to experience success with proper support in place. For example, during math, some students are working independently on problem-solving by acting out word problems and using manipulatives to solve it in their own way, some students are working closely with the teacher on understanding one-to-one correspondence, and some students are working in a group with place value manipulatives and work mats. Everyone is getting what they need. It's *differentiated* instruction.

Different instruction would be the same skill for all but with different expectations. Some students do all the problems on a page. Some students do half, and some students do ten problems. Decreasing the number of problems for students that need extra support does no good. It lowers the standard of a skill that they may not be ready to do. I've done this in the past. I've thought I provided accommodations by giving a student who struggled with addition only 7 problems instead of 15. Reducing the amount of what they needed to do didn't solve the problem. What we need to do is find out why they are struggling with addition. What if they needed counting skills forward and backward? What if they needed one-to-one correspondence? That has to come before adding.

Differentiated instruction meets learners where they're at, providing explicit instruction, and expecting excellence.

WIN (WHAT I NEED) TIME

WIN time programmed into a daily schedule for usually 30 minutes is a wonderful way to meet *all* students' learning needs. Some students need extra time for reading practice for the day, so that is what they do. Some students need extra time for writing, so they do that for the day. Some students do word work skills. Some students meet with the teacher and refine their reading skills or writing skills. Some students complete an unfinished research project, and some students work on math. For 30 minutes a day, each student is working on what they personally need. I created a chart with the aforementioned skill categories. Each day, I placed an index card with the student's name under the category the student needed to work on. Students loved this time to focus on their needs, and I loved seeing them grow in the specific areas they needed most.

WIN time is an impactful way to meet students' learning needs. WIN time doesn't change, but what students do during the time changes daily based upon their current needs.

TRIPLE-A STRATEGY

Try using the *Triple-A Strategy* for meeting the emotional and learning needs of your students.

- *Acknowledge*—Acknowledge them as a person. Get to know them. Build a relationship. Acknowledge how they are feeling. Acknowledge their learning needs.
- *Assist*—Assist them in every way you can to help them succeed. Match lessons to their developmental stages and learning needs. Find ways to meet their emotional needs. Find ways that accommodate their learning needs without lowering expectations and standards.
- *Add Awesome*—Be extra. Bring in volunteers for struggling students. One time, I took a video of myself reading and tracking print to help a student learn to track print (my first grader asked for it, so I took his advice). Yes, it took time. Yes, it was only for him, but guess what? It worked. Add awesome. Go the extra mile to be their warrior.

SOME SIMPLE STRATEGIES

Remember to constantly roam the room. No matter the age of your students, proximity is key. Proximity is enlightening for ongoing informal assessment. Proximity helps students stay engaged, but most of all, proximity allows you to provide immediate feedback on-the-spot. Roaming enables encouragement, personalized assistance, and redirection on-the-spot. Amazingly, proximity provides precise intervention for all learners' needs. It's a simple, doable strategy that is often forgotten. Remember to roam.

Be consistent. Most students thrive in a learning environment that has a posted schedule with clear expectations and follow through. A consistent schedule is predictable, providing security. Always foreshadow any schedule changes you know about and that are within your control. This helps students go with the flow.

Ask yourself: How do my students learn best? Be sure to incorporate collaboration, critical thinking, arts integration, and open-ended projects into your lessons and learning culture. Project-based-learning lends itself to life-applicable learning. Life applicable learning sticks and meets students' needs. As stated earlier, allow for movement through stations or gallery walks or breaks.

Think about how you propose questions to students. Instead of asking: Do you have any questions? (and getting deer-in-the-headlight stares.) Try: What questions do you have about...? It's a small shift that makes a *huge* difference. Students actually ask questions about the topic and don't feel afraid to ask.

REFLECTION & RESULTS

 "We do not learn from our experience. We learn from reflecting on our experience."

I agree with John Dewey. Reflection and action make a difference.

Have you ever heard the following quote often attributed to Albert Einstein? *"The definition of insanity is doing the same thing over and over and expecting different results."* Time dedicated to an endeavor doesn't necessarily equate experience. Once there was a woman who taught the same thing day in and day out for 20 years. When asked about what she did differently based on reflection, she was stumped. She didn't have 20 years' experience; she had one that she repeated 20 times. Reflection is essential for effective results and growth. Results require reflection. Reflection informs us what to keep and what to change.

Reflecting on *what* we teach is just as important as *how* we teach. Be reflective to reach all kids. Reflect on what to teach based upon needs. Reflect on how to increase engagement. Each set of kids has unique interests and needs. Find out how to tap into their interests through listening and reflecting. Then, unlock any stumbling blocks with tailored learning experiences. Reflect on your attitude and energy. How did it affect learning today? Do you need more energy? Less energy, zen? Our vibe translates into our class's behavior and attitude.

You and I need to do more than show up for kids, plan for kids, and engage kids. We need to reflect on the purpose of every single thing we do for kids. Then, we need to readjust and change for the greatest learning impact. Let's reap the rewards for the time we give. Reflect. Change if necessary. No one really likes change, but it's the catalyst to something better as long as it's backed with a plan.

It's important to let students reflect on what they've learned. Give them time to debrief each lesson. Give them time to share likes, learns, and celebrations. Permit them to share what they didn't like or what they think didn't go well. No strings attached. Reflection brings more meaning and purpose to what they are doing. It gets results. Their work has value. Reflecting on student work in portfolios reminds you and them of the effort to get to where they're at now was worth it. Reflecting also allows for growth. Keep what went well. Tweak what didn't go well. Listen to what students need to grow and do it.

It's often a challenge to have enough time to debrief; however, valuable learning is lost without it. During the debrief, students learn from each other. During the debrief, you find out what students *really* know. It can guide your future instruction. For example, I now teach STEM to over 700 students in a week. We have only 45 minutes together once a week for each class. I'm always crunched for time. But, I do my best to be intentional about debriefing each lesson. One day during a class debrief, I learned the students needed tape for their prototype success. So you better believe the next class got tape. Such a simple and easy way to meet learner needs. Sometimes, debrief allows me to know how to meet student needs for success.

One of my students' favorite ways to debrief is to use an anchor chart with three choices: square, triangle, and circle. It's a visual tool where they select a shape and complete the following statements:

- I chose a square. I learned....
- I chose a triangle. One thing I'd change is....
- I chose a circle. I'm still wondering...

We all discover what was learned and how to move forward. Students love to reflect on their learning through debriefing.

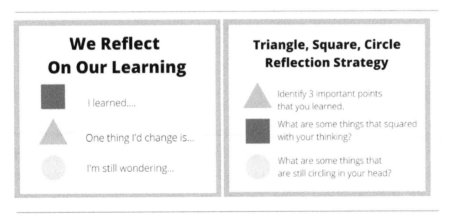

This is the chart I use for 1st- 3rd graders. Young children need the sentence starters.

This chart is for older learners.

Every day, reflect on the day's learning and listen to students. Repeat what went well and adjust what didn't. Every day reflect upon your teaching/leading. How are you meeting students' needs? How are you creating the culture you desire? What went well? What can you improve? Remember, reflection is only worth it when you apply changes for results. Reflect. Reflect. Reflect.

Meet *all* learners' needs through assessment, engaging lessons, understanding diverse cultures, allowing diversity, and differentiating lessons. Meet every single student's needs through different learning modalities. Use methods that meet their needs without lowering expectations. Help *all* students succeed and be their warrior.

NEXT STEPS:

1. What will you do tomorrow that you may not already be doing to meet your students'/school's needs?
2. Who can you partner with for a mentor/peer-tutoring relationship?
3. What will you do to add some fun to your day that leads to higher student engagement?
4. How will you ensure you hear student reflections on their learning?

CONNECT:

Connect with other warrior teachers and share what you do on Twitter or Instagram. **Share what reflection tools you use for yourself and your students to increase learning. Share what you do to keep kids engaged.** Your stories and pictures may be just what someone needs for encouragement to be a warrior for their students. You make a difference. Let's create a community, a movement amplifying *all* students. Use the hashtag #BeTheirWarrior.

CULTIVATE A CULTURE THAT PROVIDES CLEAR EXPECTATIONS

 You get what you expect and inspect what you expect.

— W. EDWARDS DEMING

irm. Consistent with high expectations. Those words swirled around my synapses and sequestered my soul. I received and perceived them as unfavorable when a well-meaning person aimed them at me. But the truth is: I am firm. I am *firm but fair,* as the adage goes. I *do* have high expectations because I know students rise to them. They become what we expect. And encourage, especially with love and scaffolding.

The person who uttered those words probably meant no harm. That's the beauty. Those uttered words caused me to reflect upon my practice. In fact, I inquired directly to the source: "Do I appear too harsh?" Quite the contrary was the reply. She witnessed I expected *all* students (including inclusion students) to meet and exceed class and lesson expectations. I assured her *all* students could do what was expected. In fact, *all* students can do what *you* expect, given the support they need. Build up your learners. Help and encourage them to be all they can be.

A week later, I was validated by our school's instructional coach: "You have great classroom management, and I saw you call on *all* students equally. Thank you for providing equity for *all* students and an equal voice." Wow! Isn't that what we all strive for? When we're intentional, we reach *all* students.

When I taught a general education class, I used call sticks. I put each student's name on a popsicle stick and put them all in a can. I'd randomly selected a stick to call on students. This prevented me from always calling on the same students, and it prevented me from calling on students who raised their hands first. Now, I teach STEM to 29 classes, which is over 700 students a week. For obvious reasons, I don't use call sticks. But I am purposeful about who I select. I always call on students that need to talk. After that, I always switch things up to include quiet students. This helps *all* students to be on their toes. They listen better because they never know when they will be called on to contribute. Quiet students who often slip through the cracks confidently share because of a loving, caring environment. Love strips fear. They take a risk. So be sure to be intentional about your expectations for *all* students. All means *all*.

High expectations begin by believing in *every* student. Regardless of their background or ability, believe in them. No matter what.

Now that I think about it, those words firm, fair, and consistent were a compliment. Kids, all people, crave structure, and boundaries. For instance, when I have extended time off during the summer, I tend to accomplish less because of the unstructured, carefree schedule. On the other hand, I tend to accomplish more with a structured work-week schedule and definite defined goals and work periods. Surely our students are no different.

I remember when my oldest son was just eight months old. Only crawling. All the baby "How To" books and experts of the era certainly would cringe with what I'm going to share next. Yep. He got his first swat to the hand.

I instructed my 8-month-old son not to touch a certain house plant. He crawled over to it. Pointed and squeaked, "Eeee?" I responded, "Yes. That is not for you." After his clarifying question, he defiantly grabbed it. He knew exactly what he was doing. He was testing his boundaries. A quick swat to his chubby little hand reminded him not to cross them. And...he never did again. (At least not that boundary.)

That 8-month-old boy who pleaded for a swat with his actions is a beloved human by most everyone he meets because of his loyalty and integrity. He fast-tracked his way in the work world because he is a caring, responsible, reliable human. He's a citizen we all hope to raise. In fact, that is what we get to do in education: raise caring, responsible, productive citizens. I'm certainly not encouraging swatting, but I am encouraging boundaries, consistency, and consequences. Our students need boundaries and clear expectations.

Actions have consequences. When you choose to do the "right" thing, you have positive consequences. When you choose not to do what is expected, you have negative consequences. The whole world spins this way.

It is essential to role model our expectations for students and not sway. Stay consistent. When students act out and push our "buttons," respond with a calm, neutral voice. Respond with consistency. When our learners know what to expect, no matter what, it equates to security. When our learners know that we will support them to reach our expectations no matter what, it equates care.

When we follow through on less than desirable behavior with pre-communicated consequences, we show we care enough to follow through. Be sure the consequences are clearly understood by students so they have a connection between their action and the consequence. For example, if a student scribbles on the table and floor, they need to clean it up. Their action of drawing on inappropriate material is followed up with a natural consequence. The action is further reinforced by stating the objects they can use to to draw on. Only when a student sees the connection and value between their behavior and a consequence will they know how to change. When we praise desirable behavior and follow through with pre-communicated rewards, it shows we care for them as humans.

Firm, fair, and high expectations backed with consistency creates a safe environment. Predictability equals security. Most students thrive in structured environments with clear expectations (I know I do).

BEHAVIOR IS COMMUNICATION

All behavior is a way of communication. Good behavior and inappropriate behavior communicates a message. When others want to blame behavior on a young, single parent or home life, I have to reject those thoughts. It's my job to positively impact the eight hours I have a student, even if it means helping parents get connected and gain resources to enhance parenting skills.

One time I heard someone comment about parents not caring enough to read with their children. Yes. It is true sometimes, but what are *we* going to do to help the child read? What are we going to do to help a student behave appropriately? We can't control their home life, but we can control what we do. Some parents are in survival mode doing the best they can. So, we need to capitalize on the time we do have with students. We need to think about what's possible, not what's impossible. Hence, students believe Audrey Hepburn's words, *"Nothing is impossible, the word itself says 'I'm possible'!"*

Help students believe in themselves and navigate negative behavior. Figure out what they are truly trying to communicate; then you'll find the root of the behavior. When you know the root, you can redirect.

Students don't wake up thinking: *I'm going to be challenging today.* Chances are high they have unmet basic needs. Negative behavior seeks approval, attention, and affirmation. They want to know if you care even when they act out. The adage: *Negative attention is better than no attention* is true. Seek to understand the behavior rather than be understood (with adults too).

I love the notion of assuming positive intent of others. For example, a student kept talking while I was giving instructions. It was driving me crazy. I wanted to yell, "Stop it!" Instead, I calmly asked the student what was going on. They informed me they were talking to get the directions repeated because they couldn't hear. I moved them closer to me. Problem solved. They quit talking while I was talking. If I hadn't assumed positive intent, I would have had a much different demeaning outcome. Find out the root cause of the behavior and work to modify it in positive ways. Give students the tools they need to communicate and express their needs. This helps them respond appropriately to situations rather than act inappropriately. Continue to praise positive behavior and growth even when students may strip it away with a negative response. In time, their needs will be met, and they'll live up to your expectations. It takes repetition and patience. Lots of patience. Remember the words by W. Somerset Maugham, "*It's a funny thing about life; if you refuse to accept anything but the best you very often get it.*"

Cultivating a positive, caring culture helps students navigate their academic and behavior challenges in productive ways. Love, accountability, and consistency keep students engaged and learning; they strive to make better choices. All students seek attention and approval. Some do it in the most distracting, irritating ways. Let's be sure to give them the skills they need and positive input, so they rise to a positive picture of themselves. Trouble maker isn't in our vocabulary or their trajectory. Students become what we expect.

DISCIPLINE IS LOVE

No one likes the word discipline. But it is life. It's necessary. I wouldn't be able to transfer these words to you without discipline. It takes self-discipline to carve out time to write. It takes self-discipline to do all things like wake up and go to work when your alarm goes off, and you'd rather stay in bed because it's a rainy, gloomy day. Discipline isn't a negative word even though we tend to think it is. Without it, we wouldn't achieve anything (or get out of bed). Let's lead our learners to success by helping them understand and practice it. One way I model love through discipline is by guiding learners who select inappropriate behavior:

1. Stop inappropriate behavior.
2. Model and teach the appropriate behavior.
3. Redirect and permit to begin applying the appropriate behavior by stating, "You may begin."

This takes time to talk through and guide students through situations. But it works most of the time (even with challenging students).

Remember, too, that sometimes behavior gets worse before it gets better. Some students strip away positive reinforcement. They don't believe they are good or deserve to be treated well. Keep modeling and redirecting. Keep loving. It builds trust. Praise desired outcomes. Catch students doing something right and specifically praise and state the appropriate action. They will do it again and again. Rather than seeing challenging students as problems, see them as opportunities.

RELATIONSHIPS & CONSISTENCY

Relationships and a positive, caring culture are number one. Every single time. However, they must be followed up by expectations and boundaries. Connection is key, but boundaries, expectations, consequences, and consistency provide security. And by providing those things, we free up time to connect rather than redirect inappropriate behavior. As an adult, I live with multiple boundaries: I must drive the speed limit, I must arrive to work on time, I must pay my bills, I must follow through when I say, "Yes." If I don't do these, I experience negative consequences wrecking my reputation. On the other hand, when I follow through, I experience positive consequences and a reputable reputation. We have a choice. Always.

Therefore, we've got to raise and teach our learners to function with the realities of the world. We have a choice to raise them to thrive or dive. So, we've got to set boundaries and reinforce them with consequences. These are societal norms. Being consistent cultivates better behavior, builds trust, and allows learners to rise to expectations.

NURTURE VERSUS EXPECT

Wouldn't it be crazy to expect babies to talk when they've never heard one spoken word? Sometimes I think we expect our students to do what we think they can do but haven't had the background experience yet to do it. We must model what we expect. We've got to scaffold those that need extra support on the way. Some will get what we model instantaneously. Others need what feels like 100s upon 100s of reinforcements. Isn't that why we're educators? To teach. Sometimes I forget that simple fact.

From time to time, I need to evaluate my own attitude toward students. Am I exasperated? How do I inspire despite exasperation? I always need to remember to believe, love, model, nurture and propel students. Sometimes I get stuck in the following mindset: *I told you once, so you should know.* But they don't. Just keep showing them until it sticks. After all, I'm *that* student. I need multiple demonstrations, reminders, and attempts. But when I get it, it sticks. Forever. Should we do anything less for our learners?

Some students feel bad when they don't do what is expected. It should be our mission to scaffold them to success. I never want a learner to leave school feeling "I'm dumb." Not on my watch. I'll scaffold them until they have success—every time.

Teach and role model what it takes to be a G.R.E.A.T. citizen. Expect G.R.E.A.T. Our school models and teaches G.R.E.A.T.

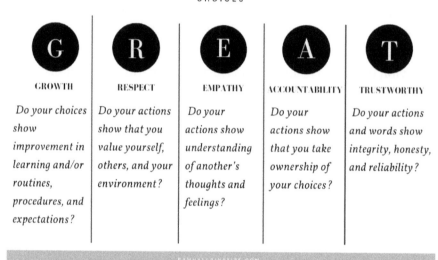

BE G.R.E.A.T.

GREAT CITIZENS MAKE GREAT CHOICES

G	R	E	A	T
GROWTH	RESPECT	EMPATHY	ACCOUNTABILITY	TRUSTWORTHY
Do your choices show improvement in learning and/or routines, procedures, and expectations?	*Do your actions show that you value yourself, others, and your environment?*	*Do your actions show understanding of another's thoughts and feelings?*	*Do your actions show that you take ownership of your choices?*	*Do your actions and words show integrity, honesty, and reliability?*

Image by Pamela Hall. Source: Isle of Wight County Schools, Smithfield, Virginia, USA

Trust is the key to relationships. It's important to create a culture built on trust. One way to instill trust is to put students in positions to prove themselves trustworthy. For example, I had a student who bolted out of our classroom daily and ran the halls. One day, before he could bolt, I gave him permission to go to the sensory hallway and touch the various sensory fabrics. He was fixated on going. Different thinking minds can't let go of an idea sometimes. I could either say "no" and create a power struggle and a running-the-halls student, or I could allow him to rise to my expectations, an opportunity to be trustworthy.

After clearly modeling and explaining expectations, I told him to go to the sensory hall and return in ten minutes. He happily skipped out the door with a timer in hand. Meanwhile, a colleague criticized me for letting him leave the classroom alone based upon his previous bolting-the-room history. She saw it as a safety hazard. I'm truly grateful for her concern. But you see, giving him the chance to leave with clear expectations of what to do and when to return set him up for success. After ten minutes, he returned. He proved to be trustworthy. You better believe I made a big deal of it in front of his peers. I bet you can guess the ending of this story? Yep. He quit bolting. He asked to leave instead, and I obliged because he could be trusted. I believe in Scudder N. Parker's words: *"People have a way of becoming what you encourage them to be."*

Being GREAT is part of our classroom and school culture. It's talked about and taught in every class throughout our building. It's expected. We're developing outstanding citizens by teaching them what it takes to be GREAT, holding them accountable, and being consistent with what we expect.

ROUTINES AND PROCEDURES ARE PARAMOUNT

Often, we start the beginning of the school year with a focused mindset for clear procedures. We're excited and pumped about a new year. Then, November hits.

So many other demands arise. We forget to follow through because we are distracted by the demands and reality of accomplishing them. That's when we have to step back and remember to follow through. Inspect what you expect. Reflect. What are you communicating with your actions? Are you overlooking your expectations? Are you reteaching them? We know that everyone needs to hear and see what you expect time and time again. Still, sometimes we forget to be consistent and repetitive. I'd love it if this were true: *I told you, so you should know.* The human brain needs to hear things multiple times for it to be a sealed deal.

I once heard that students identified as gifted and talented need to hear something new seven times. A student who is considered average needs to hear something new 21 times. A student identified with learning differences needs to hear something new over 100 times. We've got to remember that our classrooms and schools are filled with *all* types of learners. We've got to repeat and rehearse expectations over and over. Then students will rise.

What are you doing that might trigger certain behaviors? What are you reinforcing by lack of consistency? Are you giving more attention to negative behavior than positive behavior? Academically, are students gently reminded to redo and improve work to rise to expectations, or are you accepting less than their best? Maybe you need to go back to the basics.

Our routines and procedures reinforce our expectations and give students a sense of security. Sometimes, most times, they need to be revisited throughout the year.

EXPECT EXCELLENCE, BUT DON'T EVER FORGET WHAT IT FEELS LIKE TO BE A LEARNER.

Never forget the learning curve. When I lived in Germany, I learned German. (Not very well, by the way.) Each week, I'd have coffee with a German friend who taught me conversational German. Some words stuck like glue in my brain, and others seemed to exit my brain with every exhale. It was challenging. I needed multiple reminders and repetition. I was a toddler in an adult body, learning a new language. (Toddlers pick up faster, though.) Experiences like this helped me empathize with students and remember that everything is hard at first. It takes time and practice.

Another time, I took a community college sign language class.

This was *not* a good experience. (Don't be *that* teacher.) I needed help putting words to the signs the teacher was signing. Imagine a total language immersion experience in silence—just American Sign Language (ASL), with no visuals to connect to the sign. I was frustrated. My teacher didn't and wouldn't help. I got so frustrated. I eventually dropped out because I could learn better from searching the internet. This experience was good for me, though. It taught me (again) what it feels like to be a learner.

When our students are frustrated, support them, and work with them through the process. Remind them that learning is a process.

Recently, we got two adorable, wiggly, playful puppies. Puppies chew on everything—even their masters. My husband was allowing the puppies to nibble on his hands and ears. They drew blood with their sharp puppy teeth. He didn't discipline them. When the puppies were in my care, they tried to nibble on me, but I popped them on the nose with my hand stating firmly, "No!" I rewarded them with positive affirmations and a kind tone of voice when they quit nipping and biting and began licking me. Quickly, they learned to lick me when they were in my care. They acted differently around me than my husband based upon different expectations. Remember to inspect what you expect because you get what you expect.

Expect *all* learners to produce high-quality work to demonstrate what they know. One way to guide learners to produce high quality work is through allowing time to revise their work. Provide opportunities for kind, helpful, and specific feedback from peers and you with time to refine the work. *Austin's Butterfly*, found on YouTube, is an amazing example of what kids can do with constructive feedback. It's a process taking time, but the results are outstanding. It's a process of making quality work versus quantity of work a priority. Recently, it took me five rewrites and more time than I remember to produce a thirty-second video. No one wants to edit, but editing produces excellence.

A culture created for *all* learners' needs is infused with high academic and behavior expectations backed by support.

NEXT STEPS:

1. How do you inspect what you expect? How can you be more intentional about being consistent with your expectations?
2. What are your learners communicating with their behavior? What will you do tomorrow that you may not already be doing to meet your students' behavior needs?
3. What inappropriate behavior are you inadvertently feeding either through giving it attention or not following through? How will you stay consistent?
4. What will you do to reinforce desired behavior?

CONNECT:

Connect with other warrior teachers and share what you do on Twitter or Instagram. **Share how you inspect what you expect and create a culture with clear expectations that meet every single student's needs and the results.** Your stories and pictures may be just what someone needs for encouragement to be a warrior for their students. You make a difference. Let's create a community, a movement amplifying *all* students. Use the hashtag #BeTheirWarrior.

PRINCIPLE 2: COMMUNITY

Cultivate relationships meeting *all* students' needs.

James Comer states, "*No significant learning can occur without a significant relationship.*"

Community creates a sense of belonging, acceptance, and ownership, which is conveyed through culture. Culture creates spaces and places to cement relationships and build a community. Relationships connect the community.

The byproduct of a caring culture is a community of learners who want to be together no matter a student's socio-economic background or race. Relationships create a community where our learners, families, and colleagues think, "Hey, I'm not alone," or "There are others with struggles just like me," or "Someone really believes in me enough to help me." In a community, they receive emotional connections and support. In a community, they thrive.

Since no significant learning takes place without relationships, we've got to be intentional about establishing authentic relationships with our learners, our colleagues, our learners' families, and our community (town or city) partners. We need to connect our learners to their peers, so they establish relationships with each other. Many times students' relationships with each other are what keeps them coming to school.

HUMANS CRAVE RELATIONSHIPS. MAKE THEM REAL.

Dopamine. Sounds enticing, huh? It's addicting. It's the culprit enchanting and enticing people to be phone attached. Recently, I went to lunch with my hubby. We sat savoring our sandwiches and conversation. I truly think our time together put an extra pep in my step. We all crave intimacy, often replacing it with material objects and gadgets. Nothing fulfills like time with family or friends.

While we were eating, I saw an all too familiar scene: another couple waiting for their food, but they weren't conversing. They were both entranced and fixated on their phones. Why? Dopamine.

Dopamine is known as the feel-good neurotransmitter—a chemical that ferries information between neurons. The brain releases it when we eat the food we crave, contributing to feelings of pleasure and satisfaction. The chemical seeking reward system keeps us motivated to move through our world, learn, and survive. It boosts mood, motivation and attention, and helps regulate emotional responses (Sussex, n.d.). So dopamine has its place for helping us survive, but like everything, it has a down side. Addiction.

Many people crave the instant gratification of a text message and social media responses. Even if they generate a false sense of relationships and approval through likes, follows, and retweets, the gratification feels good. It's affirming. The responses give us pleasure and satisfaction; they increase our dopamine. When our seeking pleasure system is rewarded through instant gratification, we desire more and more and more.

I've been there. I've checked my phone repeatedly after posting something seeking approval and satisfaction. Sounds silly when I write it. But I chose not to stay stuck there. I call dopamine out. Social media masquerades as the real deal, but it doesn't replace a real relationship. There's no substitute.

All learners, no matter the age or background, seek relationships. Unfortunately, some seek them in unhealthy ways. So, it's up to you and me to make genuine, positive relationships a priority. Help our learners get a dopamine high from real relationships.

All our learners will show up for real, positive connections. When they show up, connect with them, connect them to others, and teach them. When we do, our students learn to cope, communicate, share emotions,

> "Social media masquerades as the real deal, but it doesn't replace a real relationship. There's no substitute."

and be authentic. They learn invaluable life skills. Even our most challenging students learn skills needed to function in a community. Making community and relationships a priority, meets learners' basic needs and frees them to learn academically. Rita Pierson stated, "*Kids don't learn from people they don't like.*" A caring culture and community precedes achievement.

No disrespect intended. However, I don't think building a community can be marginalized into six to nine weeks of lesson plans. Most education books about best practices tout the importance of team building activities in the first six to nine weeks of school to create a strong community of learners. They are absolutely correct. But it doesn't stop there. Team building isn't exclusive to the first six weeks of school. In fact, it's important to do team building activities after a long break to strengthen your community. When your students start arguing or nitpicking each other, it is time to infuse team building into lessons. By doing this periodically and consistently, your students keep a strong bond, and you keep your community strong. Remember Newton's Laws? Nothing stays the same. We're either moving forward or backward. Be intentional about community building and propel forward.

Did you ever have a time you felt left out? Capture that feeling. Let's not ever forget what it's like. Continually create opportunities for *all* learners to be included.

Since I've moved around the world, I tend to always welcome newcomers. My experience allows me to empathize exponentially. I know what it feels like to be a newcomer and feel left out. Work at making everyone feel welcome. Work at including everyone. It builds relationships. It creates a community. This next section is filled with cultivating relationships to form a community. Belonging, again.

I believe we're created to have a strong, personal bond with each other to grow together, laugh together, and play together. Classmates, neighbors, coworkers, family members—friendships develop at all levels and stages of life. This is a community.

According to James Comer, "*With every interaction in a school, we are either building community or destroying it.*" What are you doing to ensure you are building a community?

Our only hope for students and changing the world is to work together. When we work together, our small impact becomes a big impact. We need community. We're wired for

> **"School isn't a place. It's people."**

it. Our students need community; it's cultivated and expanded through unwavering relationships. Make it your mission to cultivate such strong relationships students think, *School isn't a place. It's people.*

8

RELATIONSHIPS WITH EACH CHILD

Relationships with each child are key to a positive, caring culture; it creates community.

"We don't ever age out of someone believing in us." Author Jon Acuff (2018) nailed the core of relationships in this quote. Relationships begin by believing in someone and truly taking an interest in them. I hope someone comes to mind right now that has believed in you and helped you along your journey. We get to be a warrior for *all* the learners placed in our paths. We get to build relationships with them and let them know they are loved. It all begins with a smile, being sincere, and belief.

I had the privilege of teaching a student who was deaf. He was a bright student with an electric smile and bright red hair. He lived in a silent world but expressed himself with a vivid voice through American Sign Language (A.S.L.), drawings, and gestures. Our relationship began with a smile, and I sincerely liked him. I wanted him to feel accepted and special. I wanted him to feel like part of our classroom family.

The first thing I did to build a relationship with him was to learn A.S.L. I wanted him to know I cared about him enough to communicate with him in his language. Yes, he arrived to class daily with a sign language interpreter who navigated him through lessons and the content of a frenzied first-grade schedule. But also, I wanted to be able to communicate with him—just him and me. So, I learned A.S.L. to converse with him. (Obviously, not through the community college class I dropped out of.) I loved hearing about his motorcycle and dog, Simbad. Just as important, the sign language interpreter taught the whole class daily sign language lessons so the students could communicate with him. The students loved it and befriended him. The lessons allowed the class to learn A.S.L. to "talk" at recess, during class discussions, and partner work. We *all* learned A.S.L. to strengthen our relationship. It was powerful and beautiful.

Community is created by meeting people's unique needs and building relationships. Believing in *all* students is the core of steadfast and authentic relationships that yield high student achievement. Build bridges with *all* students and break down barriers.

One day, my red-headed student's mom informed me with tears streaming down her face that she was so proud to hear her son stood in front of the class and shared what he had written in his journal for the day. You see, I thought everyone included *all* children in all things; therefore, I was puzzled she was so happy her son stood in front of the class and shared his work. Come to find out, at his previous school, the teacher had him sitting alone. She didn't expect him to share with the others because he was deaf. Honestly, I was stumped. I know that we all want what is best for our students. Maybe his previous teacher didn't realize we get what we expect and the power of relationships.

That conversation with his mom led to 100s and 100s as we forged a friendship. To this day, I still get Christmas cards from the family. I'm honored to be friends with the sign language interpreter, student, and family. True friendships surpass time, experiences, and distance.

An unwavering, life-changing relationship isn't established overnight. It took time to invest in my student and the family. We were intentional about spending time together. I was fortunate enough to

> **"The power of relationships trumps all educational endeavors."**

"loop" up to second grade with my first-grade class, including him. In that second year, relationships were solidified for life. We truly were like family. Many of those students still stay in touch with me. I'm honored and reminded the power of relationships trumps all educational endeavors.

Our relationship extended beyond school and years. Even though my friend, his past sign language interpreter, and I lived in different states from him when it was time for him to graduate, we were there. It was a tear-jerking, abs-sore-from-laughing, and reminiscing reunion. When he received honors on graduation night, I think we sat in our seats as tall and proud as his parents. We'd helped him overcome many obstacles in the two brief years we got to be a part of his life, but the ripple effect was immeasurable. Seeing him receive honors was a highlight, but I don't think it was nearly as rewarding as when he drove us through the Starbucks drive-thru. Can you picture it? A deaf young adult driving a sporty car packed with his past first-grade teacher and sign language interpreter ordering our drinks, paying for them, and driving. What a feat. How thrilling to see him be a champion!

RELATIONSHIPS LEAD TO POSITIVE CHANGE

Remember the story I share in chapter two about JJ? It was the story about my skirt being nearly up to my ears as I assisted a student whirling furniture through the air. It happened while my student teacher was taking in the whole scenario bug-eyed. He had asked me what I was going to do. I replied, "I don't know yet. I've got to get to know him and learn about him." Fast forward.

By the time the second semester rolled around, I'd had plenty of time to observe my *challenging* student in action and learn his triggers. Each day, I spent time conversing with him about his interests, which built trust. Each day, I responded to his meltdowns and throwing furniture fits with a calm, neutral voice and consistent consequences. Each day, I helped him navigate a world that seemed too big for him to fit in. Each day, I helped him communicate with peers when words seemed foreign, and fighting felt comfortable. Each day, I was there for him. Each day, I helped him calm down and breathe and cope. Each day his outbursts decreased. Because we built a relationship, he wanted to make better choices and follow my directions; he wanted to please me. Because we built a relationship, I no longer saw furniture flying across the room. Relationships resonate with a powerful message: I care about you. You matter.

I studied how he reacted in certain situations to meet his emotional and learning needs. It's part of our culture, but when we follow through and meet needs, it seals the deal and creates a real relationship.

I learned he was sensitive to sound. So one day, to stop his obsessing about the sound and to avoid a meltdown, I had him put cotton in his ears. It worked. After that, I sought out noise-blocking headphones.

After much invested time, JJ greeted me with a smile instead of a scowl. He presented me with pictures he'd drawn of him and me together. When we build relationships, believe in our students, and meet their needs, we're their warrior.

RELATIONSHIP BUILDING BASICS

- **Listen.** "Listen" and the word "silent" have the same letters in them. Sometimes you need to be silent to truly listen to others. Stopping and listening send the message: You are worthwhile.
- **The teacher's attitude translates to the students' attitudes.** Keep your attitude in check. Remember, what we do is more powerful than what we say. Attitudes are caught, not taught.
- **Be consistent.**
- **Be fair.**
- **Explain all actions, so learners know the reason behind the response.**
- **Listen to their stories and share your stories.**
- **Play frisbee or whatever they like to play during recess.** Swing on the swings with them. Shoot hoops.
- **Eat lunch with them.** This is treasured time. Bond over food.
- **Give the gift of time.** Spend time with them.
- **Be present.** I used to get so caught up in how things looked and preparing meals for people who came to our house that I forgot just to be present. I planned, prepared, scrubbed, and served. I ran around anxiously, asking everyone what they needed. My husband said one time after a gathering at our house, "Stop running around and working to make everything perfect. You're making guests feel uncomfortable." He was right. People come for connection. Sure, the food needs to taste good, and your home needs to be presentable. But that's it. Let the rest go. Relax. Do dishes after people leave. Sit with everyone. Be present. How does this story translate to students? Be in the

moment. Forget about your task lists and bazillion preparations that need to be done.

Being present is a present,
a gift. Give it to all, not just
students.

- **Give birthday gifts and birthday messages.**
- **Find out what makes them tick.** Talk to them about it and supply them with resources for their interests. For example, if a student loves horses and you have horse books, give the horse books to them. It seems so common sense but is often overlooked because of our demanding schedules.
- **Have open communication.**
- **Smile.** Always.
- **Be sincere.**
- **Admit when you're wrong.**
- **Ask for forgiveness.**
- **Validate students' perspective.**
- **Ask questions like:** Tell me more, how did you do that? How did you get that answer?
- **Every day is a fresh start. Every class period is a fresh start.**
- **Laugh together.**
- **Be silly.**

This isn't an extensive list, but it sure puts smiles on our learners' faces and cements relationships.

Try This

Be intentional about spending two minutes for 10 consecutive days talking to a student about their interests. Get to know them. Keep the conversation centered around them and not school or academics.

2 X 10 strategy is a simple strategy I learned from Angela Watson for building relationships, especially with challenging students. (Watson, 2018).

2 minutes x 10 days = Powerful Impact.

BE YOU

Being authentically you is what all students need. You are the secret sauce in their lives. I love the way Bob Burg and John David Mann authors of *The Go-Giver* (2015) sum up the concept.

 Remember this: no matter what your training, no matter what your skills, no matter what area you're in, you are your most important commodity. The most valuable gift you have to offer is you. Ninety-plus percent of relationships are people skills. And what's the foundation of all people skills? Liking people? Caring about people? Being a good listener? Those are all helpful, but they're not the core of it. The core of it is who you are. It starts with you. As long as you're trying to be someone else, or putting on some act or behavior someone else taught you, you have no possibility of truly reaching people. The most valuable thing you have to give people is yourself.

Do you want to make an impact and build unwavering relationships and community with your learners? Then, be authentically *you*.

You'll know you've created community and established a relationship when you hear the following: "I wish the weekends weren't so long. I'll miss you."

Author Josh Shipp bounced around foster care home to foster care home. Now he is a successful motivational speaker and public figure. One of his favorite sayings, "*Every kid is one caring adult away from a success story,*" rings true. Invest in your students. You have the power to be a puzzle piece to their success story. They'll love you for caring and being you.

NEXT STEPS:

1. Remember, there's no one-size-fits-all solution, strategy, method, or answer for meeting students' needs. We need to meet *all* students' needs right where they're at and figure out what works best for each one to be their warrior. What can you do tomorrow to get to know your students better?

2. Assessment is all about learning and meeting student needs; when we know their needs, we can develop a plan to meet all students' needs. What can you do tomorrow/this week to assess the emotional and academic needs of your students?

3. How will you devise a plan to meet them? (Even if you select 1-3 students, you will be doing something better today than you did yesterday to be their warrior.)

CONNECT:

Connect with other warrior teachers and share what you do on Twitter or Instagram. **Share how you intentionally build relationships with your students. Share the results.** Your stories and pictures may be just what someone needs for encouragement to be a warrior for their students. You make a difference. Let's create a community, a movement amplifying *all* students. Use the hashtag #BeTheirWarrior.

9

RELATIONSHIPS WITH EACH CHILD'S FAMILY

Create strong relationships with families. Partnerships with families
are crucial to student success.

*W*e live in a world where being busy is a badge. When
we're too busy being busy, we miss opportunities to
create community. We've got to extend love to families by being available. (Yes, we need to set boundaries for our availability, but we've got
to let them know we care.) Don't be in such a hurry teaching and with
life, you miss an opportunity to build a relationship with each child's
family.

Cultivating relationships with families leads to community cama-
raderie.

6 SIMPLE WAYS TO CULTIVATE RELATIONSHIPS WITH FAMILIES

1. Smile and be sincere
2. Listen. Extend empathy.
3. Apologize when you make a mistake. A sincere apology diffuses an angry family member.
4. Be a problem solver meeting their needs.
5. Provide resources. Some families don't know their options. We can share resources to help their family overcome a need. We can share resources that can help them provide structure for a challenging student. Sometimes families need us to be their warrior too. When we are-the child wins.
6. Communication is key.

Regular communication through multiple modes and multiple times a week provides families with information. It sends the message you truly care about them. I did the following: Daily agenda, a weekly newsletter (hard copy and electronic), positive notes home, positive phone calls home, and regular posts on an app like Bloomz. My learners' families loved using the Bloomz App because I posted pictures 2-3 times a week, making them feel connected to their child's day and learning. The App also allowed families to schedule volunteer time or to provide needed classroom supplies. It also enabled me to send out quick announcements and reminders. Many families utilized the private messaging feature too. There are several Apps educators can or do use. Choose one that works best for you.

Strong communication avoids trouble with families later. When families are informed, they have fewer questions, and they are invested in your community.

Try This

- Create positive notes to send home. I had postcards created with our class logo, website QR code, and a positive message. Since they are preprinted, sending home a positive message is simple. I add a personalized note and sign my name. The students love to get a positive postcard, especially since so much communication is digital. Families connect because they see you truly care for their child by taking the time to handwrite a note. A positive postcard can be hung up, saved, and revisited.
- Include parents in as much as possible. Invite them into your learning space frequently. Enlist them to volunteer.
- Enlist them to share their expertise. I've had family members share all kinds of lessons with students, from bringing in a large boa and teaching about reptiles to the chemistry of soap making to beekeeping to creating soil to what it's like to be an author. These encounters expose students to multiple experiences. They get hooked on something they may not have known they liked or could do. You are their warrior by enlisting others' gifts and talents for exponential exposure to experiences beyond your repertoire.

I'll never forget my oldest son's first conference. I was so eager to hear all he was learning only to be chastised for all the ways he didn't measure up to the teacher's standards. The funny thing is that my son wasn't a "problem child." She made him out to be. In fact, she spent the entire scheduled 20 minutes telling me everything that he wasn't good at. She didn't tell me one thing he did well. I left wondering what it must be like for him to spend his day saturated in a negative environment. After the conference, I was so discouraged about my sweet boy and his first school experience. I sat in a puddle of tears in my car.

At that moment, I vowed no family member of a student I taught would ever feel like that leaving my presence. (Good news. We moved my son to a different school, and he flourished. The teacher spoke of him like I knew him to be, a wonderful child with areas to grow.) Make sure to find something good to share with family members. Even if working with their child is challenging, look for something good to share. I'm sure you've heard the "sandwich approach." Tell them something good, tell them what the learner needs to work on and how, and end with something they do well. Another way to think about it is as follows: *3/1 ratio. Positive comments to "negative" in giving feedback.*

One time I had a grandmother challenge me at every crossroad about what we did in class and every time I tried to get extra help for her child. In fact, she wanted to remove her child from my class. It never materialized because he cried and convinced her to leave him in my room. He felt safe, secure, and loved. I had a relationship with her child. I worked to cultivate one with her too, but she refused. Therefore, even when you do everything possible, you may not please everyone. Don't ever stop doing what is best for kids. Keep working on *all* relationships. How others respond is out of your control.

Building positive relationships with families helps everyone through challenging times. Sometimes we have to share with families things they don't want to hear. For example, I had to share with a family that their child needed extra services. They didn't want to receive extra help for their child. Still, when they asked me to write down what I was currently doing to help their child, I compiled two double-spaced pages of accommodations. Until I sat down and wrote them out, I wasn't aware I was implementing so many accommodations for her child to succeed. Two double-spaced pages of strategies designed to meet her child's needs were poignant proof that I cared. Isn't that what we do as educators? We make multiple accommodations on the spur of the moment daily for our students; we do whatever it takes for students to succeed. (Be sure to document, document, and document everything you do.) We were nearing the end of the school year, and I wanted my student's success to continue. I wanted to ensure a system was in place so the current accommodations would continue, no matter the teacher.

Because of our relationship, the family knew I loved their child. We built trust. When it came time to share a hard truth, they were more receptive to hear what was needed for their child to succeed. Building positive relationships helps when you have to share uncomfortable facts. Because they know you care, they are more receptive. You can move forward with trust.

When I meet with families, I always sit at a circular table. I sit in a relaxed position near them with work samples. Simply sitting near them instead of across from them sends a friendly message. Our body language sends messages. I sit relaxed to put families at ease. Some families don't like coming to school because they had negative experiences. It's important to do everything possible to create a positive experience for them. Try the following when you conference with families. (I've used this recipe for years, and it works well every time. It opens up great dialogue.)

RECIPE FOR PARTNERSHIPS WITH FAMILIES

1. Regarding (insert student's name) progress so far, what are you pleased with?
2. What are we doing to create these successes?
3. What do you think could be going better?
4. What is/are your objective(s) for (insert student's name) for the next (insert a time period)? (We discuss how to make this happen.)
5. I share what the student is doing well and areas that they can display growth. I use student work to go with what I state.
6. What can I do better to meet your child's needs?
7. We always end on a happy note.

Families are one of our greatest assets. Let's do everything in our power to cultivate relationships with them, build bridges, acquire allies, and create community.

NEXT STEPS:

1. To build strong bonds with families, ask yourself: How do I want my learners' families to feel when they arrive? How do I want my learners' families to feel when they are in my

classroom? How do I want learners' families to feel when they leave? Be intentional about making your answers happen.

2. What is one thing you can do today or tomorrow to build a better relationship with your learners' families? What else can you do to create community with families so *all* students can succeed?

3. What will you do tomorrow that you may not already be doing to communicate with families?

CONNECT:

Connect with other warrior teachers and share what you do on Twitter or Instagram. **Share how you partner with families and the results.** Your stories and pictures may be just what someone needs for encouragement to be a warrior for their students. You make a difference. Let's create a community, a movement amplifying *all* students. Use the hashtag #BeTheirWarrior.

10

RELATIONSHIPS WITH THEIR PEERS

Connect students to other students by fostering friendships.

*M*ost students come to school to see their friends. Friends keep us going, friends give us worth, friends help us, friends have the power to shape our performance, and friends are our community. Friendship is often underrated, considering the tremendous impact it has on our students' well being. Friendships help develop social and emotional skills and an increasing sense of belonging while decreasing stress. Thus, we need to make connecting our students to their peers a priority and nurture our students' friendships. Developing a culture and community that fosters friendships is essential.

NEVER UNDERESTIMATE THE IMPORTANCE OF FRIENDSHIP

Two curly-headed boys who loved football became best buds. It all started when I learned through our morning meetings they both played football. When I learned they lived in the same neighborhood, I became intentional about partnering them for lessons and learning. A friendship forged. It became a pivotal friendship.

Before nurturing this friendship, one of the boys had a history of absences. For two years in a row, he'd missed more than 23 days a year. Because of this special friendship, he came to school. High absences became a thing of the past for him. When he *was* absent, his football friend informed me of his status. They bonded beyond the school walls. They were buds who brought out the best in each other.

When time is spent with morning meetings and team building activities coupled with being intentional about connecting students with common interests, friendships are bound to flourish; kids make connections with each other, which has positive peer effects. (I call it positive peer pressure.

5 POSITIVE PEER EFFECTS

1. They want to come to school.
2. They look out for each other.
3. They help each other learn.
4. They are motivated to do well because their friends are watching.
5. They increase communication and social skills.

I noticed those two curly-headed boys shared their gifts and talents. When one looked confused, the other explained what to do. Friends help each other. Friendships give everyone a sense of belonging and a desire to achieve.

CULTIVATING A COMMUNITY THAT FOSTERS FRIENDSHIPS

All kinds of lives are being transformed before my eyes in ways that can never be measured on a standardized test but matter more than a test score. It's called life. Students build relationships that are unwavering in a positive, caring culture. When you value every student, regardless of how they behave, and expound on their strengths while talking about their areas needing growth, students display empathy for others. They cheer when someone overcomes a struggle. They lend a hand when they see a student that needs to overcome a different struggle. When they have what seems like nothing but give what little they have (a chewed eraser) to a student that doesn't have an eraser, it's a win. They exhibit compassion and empathy. Students immediately help struggling students because they know what it feels like to struggle. They encourage. They applaud progress. Their kindness and empathy for each other are life skills far more important and essential than any grade or test measurement. They're exceeding in life. They are friends for what they say is forever.

Build relationships through understanding your students' thinking and allowing them to share their thinking with others. We always say, "There is more than one way to solve a problem." The students share their way so others can learn. This creates value for what they do and who they are.

There are many ways to foster friendships, but here are a few that are tried and true.

FOSTERING FRIENDSHIPS IS KEY TO ESTABLISHING A POSITIVE, CARING COMMUNITY

1. Model friendship skills and communication skills.
2. Teach "I" statements to help students communicate through conflicts. (This strategy is in chapter 5 too. I think it's worth repeating.)
   a. Example: *I feel* (insert emotion) *when you* (insert action) *because...*
      Can you please (insert what action is desired)
      Both students acknowledge feelings and take action.
3. Implement and practice the "Golden Rule": Treat other people how you want to be treated.
4. Role model and teach: Treat everyone with equal care and respect. (You don't have to like 'em. You just have to be nice to 'em.)
5. Give the gift of positive words to each other.

Giving the gift of positive words is unforgettable. Using the book *The Important Book* By Margaret Wise Brown as a model, I have students create a page for their peers for their birthday to put into a birthday book. We title the book *(Student's name) is Important.* On the day of any given student's birthday, the rest of the class writes a page for the birthday book, a book filled with positive words and illustrations that can be revisited repeatedly. The frame goes like this:

- The important thing about...(insert birthday student's name) is... (Peers write all the things that they think are special about the person. This takes up several lines of paper.)
- But the important thing about (insert birthday student's name) is...(insert something important about them. Circle it back to the opening sentence.)

Students receive the gift of kind words they can revisit again and again.

Recently a former first grader from 18 years ago sent a picture to me via social media holding their birthday book from first grade. Now, they're 24 years old! Wow! That's the power of creating a caring community, connecting peers, and positive words. (The student that sent the picture was a quiet student who may have slipped through the cracks, but because of a strong community of learners, *all* students flourished.) That same student sent a photo of themselves with a classmate from that first-grade class. Their bond lasted 18 years and continues to grow. Creating a community by connecting students to students is impactful.

Please connect your students and foster peer-to-peer friendships. For them, it's life-changing.

NEXT STEPS:

1. What is one thing you can do today or tomorrow to connect your students with each other?
2. What else can you do to create a community by connecting students to their peers so *all* students can succeed?
3. How can you incorporate an avenue for students to give the gift of positive words to their peers?

CONNECT:

Connect with other warrior teachers and share what you do on Twitter or Instagram. **Share how you promote peer-to-peer relationships and the results.** Your stories and pictures may be just what someone needs for encouragement to be a warrior for their students. You make a difference. Let's create a community, a movement amplifying *all* students. Use the hashtag #BeTheirWarrior.

11

RELATIONSHIPS WITH YOUR PEERS

Strong adult-to-adult relationships raises student achievement.

ave you ever worked in a toxic environment? One where you were afraid to speak what was really on your mind and what you truly thought was best for kids. One where colleagues were kind to your face and cutthroat behind your back. I have. It's miserable. It sucks the life out of you.

Have you ever worked where the words *all, us, our, team,* and *together* were the norm instead of the words *me, my, mine,* and *I*? A place where you felt valued and respected. A place where sharing your gifts and talents were welcomed, and your successes were celebrated—a place where teamwork was the heartbeat of the culture. I have. It brings joy and purpose.

When you strive for a common goal, it doesn't feel like work or a job. It's a passion. When the common goal is to do whatever it takes for every student to succeed, kids become the focus, and achievement escalades. The axiom Together Everyone Achieves More (TEAM) rings true. Steve Jobs, the co-founder of Apple Inc., remarked, "*My business model is The Beatles: They were four guys that kept each others' negative tendencies in check; they balanced each other. And the total was greater than the sum of the parts.*" I love this notion.

Being an educator is hard work, but it's also all about relationships. Whether we agree with each other or not isn't as important as working together and keeping each other in check for all our students' sake. It's important to work with colleagues enhancing each other's gifts and talents. When we do, our students benefit.

> "When you strive for a common goal, it doesn't feel like work or a job. It's a passion."

It's so essential to be a good colleague. Not only will it benefit your work, but it also will set a strong example for your students. In today's confrontational TV and Internet culture, children need to see adults in their world expressing collegiality, caring, and concern.

IDEAS TO BE A GOOD AND CARING COLLEAGUE

- **Communicate honest, sincere appreciation every chance you get.** Everyone, not just our students, wants to be loved, needed, appreciated and recognized.
- **Make connections with those that show compassion and passion for kids.** Work together and share ideas. Reach out to them with kindness. Offer to help them. All relationships are based on mutual give-and-take, where people selflessly work together. If all you do is take, your colleagues will stop giving. Another positive twist on this is to let your students see you help your colleagues. Children don't always do what we say, but they always watch what we do and often mimic those behaviors.
- **Complete each other instead of competing with each other.** Share what you have. Share ideas. Be willing to collaborate. You will never become less by helping others rise. Assist your colleagues in any way possible. For example, One of my colleagues was put in a school position

that I had hoped for. Instead of being upset, I helped her set up the room and provided her with current materials and resources from a conference that I had attended. The information helped her, but ultimately, it helped kids. It's always about doing what is best for *all* kids.

- **Share kids.** Have a mindset that *all* students are *your* students. It's not *your* kids versus *my* kids, but it's *our* kids. When we all work together for the good of *all* our students, the kids win. The following is an example: Every morning, my colleague and I stood outside our doors and greeted all our students. After a while, it became evident some of my students were partial to my colleague. They clicked. On the other hand, some of my colleagues' students were more attracted to me. So my colleague would take the time to seek students that were partial to her from my class to continue to build a relationship. Likewise, I did the same. Some mornings, multiple students from her room stood in line for hugs from me, and vice versa. Also, my colleague and I had fun together. We'd play music and sing and dance. We helped each other in every imaginable situation. Our students were watching. Although they weren't physically taking notes, they were absorbing our interactions. Suddenly they began to float from room to room with acts of kindness and concern for others beyond their own classroom walls. They knew we loved *all* kids, not just the ones on our class roster. Besides creating a community with my colleague, we shared our kids to meet all kids' needs.

- **Be a good listener.** I've stated it before, "listen" and "silent" have the same letters in them for a reason. Be silent. Just listen to a colleague unload their frustrations. Often, they will come up with their own solutions just by being able to vent. Affirm and encourage them. I often ask, "Do you want me to give advice or just listen?" This helps you navigate your relationship, so they want to keep sharing with you. Sometimes all you need to do is listen, and sometimes they need a nugget of your experience and expertise or your point of view. Only give advice when asked. Most of the time, they need an empathetic ear.

- **Be present.** This was shared in chapter 8, Relationships With Each Child. Still, it applies to all relationships. Be mindful of being in the moment. Silence your mental "to do" lists. Just be fully present and engaged with others.

- **Connect colleagues to support systems.** When educators feel supported, they can better extend more support to their students.

- **Be professional.** Value and respect your colleagues. Work with them.

- **Be a conduit.** No matter how hard I try, I've learned I may not "click" with all students. I do everything right, but the relationship isn't right. We don't have an affinity. That's when I'm a connector. I connect them to an adult (a colleague) that "clicks" (bonds) because it's not about me. It's *always* about reaching *all* students.

- **Partner with colleagues who inspire students.** Other people inspired some of my students in the building. I built in regular times they could spend time with them. For example, one student loved a kindergarten teacher in our building. We set up a weekly time my student could visit with the teacher and read to her class.

- **Be a culture builder, not a culture buster.** Focus on solutions, not complaining. Diffuse gossip. Role model building positive relationships.

- **Be flexible.** I once heard the following quote, and it stuck: "Blessed are the flexible for they will never be bent out of shape." Cover a colleague's class or adapt your schedule to accommodate a project or event they are doing. Being an educator is about being flexible in all circumstances daily, right? It's what we do.

- **Establish a "Tap in Tap out" system.** A "Tap in, tap out" system allows self-care. It's 10 -15 minutes of quiet time to regroup and refocus. This strategy allows you to call in support so you can step out of the room (Berger, 2018). This is a wonderful system to establish with a colleague. You take turns as needed. (I know there were multiple times I wished I could do this. It helps prevent burnout.)

- **Laugh, grow, and play together.** Set up book studies. Go to conferences together. Present professional growth sessions together. Have fun together.

- **Look for ways to serve others through Random Acts of Kindness.** Find out what they drink in the mornings. If it's coffee, stop and pick up their favorite. This is a fabulous way to start the day together.

- **Be a team player.** Teachers are often isolated in their own rooms and situations. However, studies show that strong adult-to-adult relationships for kids raises student achievement. Teams tap into talents, which ultimately affects kids. Be a team for kids. Surround yourself with a strong support system. We need each other. This is heart work. It drains us emotionally, physically, and mentally. Support helps us see solutions when we only see problems. When we continue to show up with our piece of the puzzle completed for the greater good, we build rapport and trust. Be willing to collaborate. Admit when you don't know something. We are stronger together. Support helps to refocus us on what truly matters—the kids.

- **Cling to sunshine.** Some people are storms. They seem happiest making thunder. Drama is their middle name. Stay clear from the storm. Cling to sunshine people. Cling to people who encourage you, stretch you, and bring out the best in you.

- **Relationships take time.** Invest your time in those that are like-minded and going in the direction you want to go. Relationships grow with time spent together. So remember, it takes time to foster relationships with peers, but it's worth it.

Good relationships with colleagues are important. When adults in a building get along, students notice, and achievement goes up. Additionally, your connections with colleagues play a huge role in enjoying your work and growing as a professional. Because you work with your colleagues year after year, it's likely your relationships morph into long-lasting friendships.

Imagine everyone pulling together toward a common goal and doing what's best for kids? Imagine a place filled with passion and purpose. Imagine a place where you feel free to make mistakes, take risks, and grow. It's possible. It begins with you reaching out to your colleagues and creating community. You can do it, one relationship at a time.

> "Good relationships with colleagues are important. When adults in a building get along, students notice, and achievement goes up."

NEXT STEPS:

1. What are some steps you can take tomorrow to reach out to a colleague you admire and/or a colleague who challenges you?
2. Who can you support this week with a Random Act of Kindness?

3. How can you be a conduit for your students, ensuring that *all* students' needs are met?

CONNECT:

Connect with other warrior teachers and share what you do on Twitter or Instagram. **Share how you build relationships with your peers (colleagues) in your school. What were the results?** Your stories and pictures may be just what someone needs for encouragement to be a warrior for their students. You make a difference. Let's create a community, a movement amplifying *all* students. Use the hashtag #BeTheirWarrior.

12

RELATIONSHIPS WITH THE COMMUNITY

Build bridges with community businesses and form bonds that enable students more opportunities.

*I*t's no secret that family involvement is an integral part of a successful educational framework. Numerous studies identified family engagement as a critical factor affecting all students' success and the school environment (Teach Me To Learn, 2014). But what many schools and educators overlook is that high student success is generally the result of three groups collaborating to provide the best opportunities for the future—teachers, families, and the community. In the two previous chapters, we've explored how colleagues and families working together in a community help all kids succeed. Now we'll dive into *why* and *how* we connect with our local community, which leads to student success.

I don't know what my students would do without local experts in our community. Yes, I do; they'd suffer. I love community partnerships because they offer learners far more than I can provide. Local businesses and experts expand students' experiences. They're vital. Mr. Rogers, the much-loved host of the public television show "Mister Rogers Neighborhood," wisely stated, "*Anyone who does anything to help a child is a hero to me.*" Our community experts and businesses are heroes.

Community collaboration with schools complements and reinforces values, culture, and the learning opportunities for our students. In other words, all of us—educators, families, businesses, nonprofits, service clubs, and the like—working together, truly make a difference in our students' lives.

Always be on the lookout to connect students to their community; learning goes beyond the classroom and school walls. Look at every organization as an opportunity for kids to learn. The connection may become their passion and career.

8 WAYS TO CONNECT & COLLABORATE WITH YOUR LOCAL COMMUNITY

1. **Reach out to local experts.** Be intentional about thinking that everyone has something to teach your students. Don't ever be afraid to ask them to teach your students. I've found most everyone wants to share their passion and help kids. For example, my friend and I attended a local butterfly society meeting. (I know, sounds boring, right?) It turned out to be extremely hands-on and educational. Immediately, I met the person in charge and solicited them to visit our school. Another time, my students learned all about hydroponics, greenhouse growing, and greenhouse to kitchen, to table lessons from an expert at the local culinary institute. Another time, a local 4-H extension agent taught my students how to create proper soil, check pH, germinate seeds, and so much more.

2. **Reach out to other educators in other schools in your community.** The following are some examples that have given my students opportunities:
   - A high school health and nutrition class came to our school and taught students a hands-on health and nutrition lesson. My elementary students loved connecting with high school students.
   - The high school engineering class cut out my elementary engineering class' pinewood car designs. They gave my students something to strive for--high school engineering.
   - The high school makerspace students collaborated with my elementary students on creating screen prints for the project-based learning project.

3. **View all businesses and establishments as field experience opportunities.**
   - My students engaged in life lessons from the following: local landfill (importance of recycling and sustainable career options), local soap company (chemistry and entrepreneurship), local cotton gin (farming, harvesting, textiles, marketing), grocery store, bank, post office, television station, garden nurseries, zoo, aquarium, etc.
   - My students set up a beehive, gave out informative brochures, and shared bee-friendly products at our local hardware store. It was a win-win. It brought in more business for the store, and the store displayed its bee-friendly pesticides and flowers for purchase while allowing my students to promote saving bees.
   - Everyone and every business is a learning opportunity for our students. Reach out for resources and assistance.

4. **Build bridges with local organizations.**
   - The local women's club taught my students how to make mats and blankets out of plastic bags. They donated them to organizations that support the homeless.
   - The local beekeeper association taught the entire school the importance of bees in our lives, set up a hands-on exhibit, and invited us to a bee yard.
   - The Chesapeake Bay Foundation taught our students the importance of preserving the bay through multiple avenues, including oyster gardening.
   - Many local clubs and organizations will fund projects. Just search for them and ask.

5. **Local Libraries** are packed with experts and learning opportunities for our students.

6. **Authors and storytellers** I have a favorite storyteller who focuses on diversity and multicultural stories share with my students. She captivates them in a way that's unobtainable for me. Invite local authors to share their books or meet authors from around the world through a video conference.

7. **Museums and art institutes**
   There are many, many enriching museums and art institutes that accompany a wide array of topics. If you can't go in person, there are wonderful virtual options. Just do a search to match your topic, and you'll more than likely find an enhancing experience for your learners.

8. **Bring in guests that match the heritage of your students**
   Share stories and celebrate diversity.

While the above list isn't extensive, it should get your creative juices flowing for ways to involve your community. Their expertise and excitement expose students to new resources and possibilities in life. Additionally, it gives community clubs and businesses positive public exposure, and it creates a positive relationship with your school. It's a win-win.

Be sure to have students follow up with handwritten thank you letters or cards. I know digital is dominant, but handwritten notes convey care. The point here is to follow up with some student-created "thank you" regardless if it is digital or handwritten. Let's face it; there are some super cool ways to send digital "thank yous," such as through creating a photo slide presentation or sending an Ecard.

Life applicable learning through community partnerships ignites a love of learning. When we seek out relationships with the community, our students' rewards include connections, options, mentors, diversity, leadership opportunities, awards, projects, donations, apprenticeships, and relationships with others that believe in them. These relationships make our students and schools stronger.

Community partnerships are essential for helping students achieve their maximum potential. Connecting our students to their community generates a generation of life-long learners who become passionate citizens in their community through life-applicable lessons and relationships. Community collaboration is priceless.

NEXT STEPS:

1. Brainstorm a list of local businesses, clubs, and organizations. Think about how they can expand your students' learning opportunities and experiences.
2. What are some steps you can take tomorrow to reach out to someone in your community?
3. How can you be a conduit for your students, ensuring that *all* students' needs are being met through community connections?

CONNECT:

Connect with other warrior teachers and share what you do on Twitter or Instagram. **Share how you connect your learners to local businesses, organizations, and experts in your community. What**

were the results? Your stories and pictures may be just what someone needs for encouragement to be a warrior for their students. You make a difference. Let's create a community, a movement amplifying *all* students. Use the hashtag #BeTheirWarrior.

PRINCIPLE 3: BE STRONG

Start STRONG and embrace self-care.

My forehead hit the steering wheel as I sat in my car in the school parking lot and sobbed uncontrollably. It was 1:30 PM. My students were now in math stations with a colleague as I wiped away tears. Their behavior led to my surrender. After half a day of students throwing furniture, stomping their feet and yelling "no," crawling on the floor, interrupting lessons, and the list of mayhem goes on, I picked up the phone. Crying, I informed my principal I needed to go home. I was humiliated. How did I get to this place of surrender? Why couldn't I take it anymore? Why couldn't I redirect those situations with love and compassion? Why, why, why? I condemned myself with "should haves." I should have been able to do it. I should have... But the bottom line is that I reached a place of extreme burnout. I tapped out. It took me until the spring to reach this place, but what if I'd been mindful about preparing my mind and body all along the way? What if I'd been taking care of myself better, getting more sleep, and doing what was enjoyable? Maybe just maybe I wouldn't have tapped out.

Stressed out, burned out, anxiety-filled. We've all experienced these emotions at some point in our lives. Sometimes more frequently than we'd like to admit. There's a better option: Be STRONG.

When I was on the verge of leaving education, my calling, I created STRONG. STRONG is a mindset. It encompasses self-care, but it's also about establishing habits for a healthy mind, body, and soul. I decided to be intentional about being STRONG. You can too. STRONG isn't a miracle cure all, but it will set you on the path to passion and purpose instead of the brink of burnout. It's proactive and preventive.

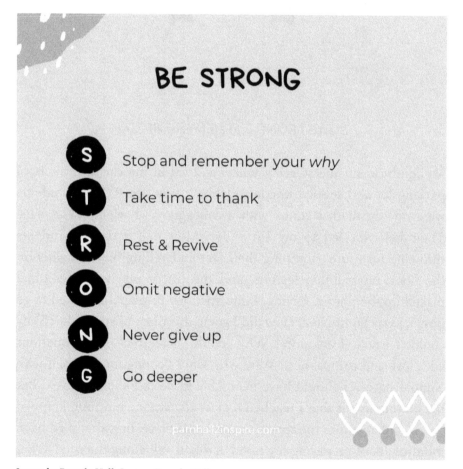

BE STRONG

S — Stop and remember your *why*

T — Take time to thank

R — Rest & Revive

O — Omit negative

N — Never give up

G — Go deeper

pamhallinspire.com

Image by Pamela Hall. Source: Pamela Hall

Start with just stopping. Slow down. Pause. Being **STRONG** involves: S-stop and remember your *why*. Then, T- take time to thank. Be thankful. Purposefully fill your thoughts with gratitude. **R**-rest and revive. All of nature has a rhythm of rest. All Olympic gold medal winners prepare to be strong for their sport, but they, too, must rest to be even stronger. Once you are rested and recharged, it is essential to **O**- omit negative thoughts and **N**-never give up on yourself or students. Remember to **G**- go deeper. Grow. Both personally and professionally. We'll dig into the details of each step in upcoming chapters in this Principle section of the book.

Have you ever heard the phrase you can't pour from an empty vessel? Benjamin Franklin puts it this way, "*When the well is dry, we know the worth of water.*"

As educators, we give and give and give every single second of every single day. It's what we do. We're givers. However, if we keep giving and giving and don't take time to fill ourselves up, what is left? Stressed out, exhausted, and burned out vessels. We all want more than that. You're meant for more.

Whether it's a runner, professional athlete, hobbyist, or student, they all prepare for their race, craft, or test. They prepare their bodies and minds. We tell our students to get more sleep and eat nutritious food before test day. Everyone who wants to perform well prepares well. We even service our vehicles, so they run at peak performance. Why is it then many educators neglect their bodies and minds? Especially when you are a vehicle to be your learners' warrior.

This book ends with this section, where we need to begin in our lives. So the end's really the beginning. I wanted to start the book with being STRONG, but my wonderful friend Angie laughed and snorted, "You can't

> **"Everyone who wants to *perform* well prepares well."**

start with that principle. No one will read your book because we all know what we are supposed to do, but we don't do it." I encourage you to start STRONG. All the kids and people you encounter are worth it. You are worth it.

Whenever I fly, I am reminded of a valuable truism. Before the plane takes off to my destination, the flight attendants do their routine checks and safety procedures. Safety procedures are so vital; they're an every flight mandate. Did you guess where this is going? It's the bit where the oxygen masks drop down from above your seat, and you're instructed to put on your mask before assisting someone else. Yes, it's cliche', but it holds significant truth: We must take care of ourselves before we can effectively take care of anyone else. (The keyword is effectively.)

As educators, we *know* we need to take care of ourselves, but we continue to put others first. So why is this? What can we do about it?

Self-care isn't self-indulgence. So often, we think it is. But unlike self-care, self-indulgent activities don't have lasting benefits. While self-care helps promote long-term health, self-indulgent habits are things like binge-watching TV or eating too much junk food, and they don't enhance our health (Waterford, 2021).

The definition of self-care is any action that you use to improve your health and well-being. According to the National Institute of Mental Illness ([NAMI], Waterford, 2021), there are six elements to self-care:

- Physical
- Psychological
- Emotional
- Spiritual
- Social
- Professional

A STRONG educator mindset encompasses the six components of self-care. As educators, self-care is essential more now than ever before for multiple reasons.

Teaching is physically, mentally, and emotionally draining. Why are teachers so mentally drained at the end of the day? You probably guessed it. Teachers make over 1500 educational decisions every school day (Goldberg & Houser, 2017). Usually more. (That's about 4 decisions every minute in a 6 hour day. We all know that our day is longer than that.) They often lie awake at night because they internalize their students' struggles and pain. Educators focus so much energy on others, leaving little to no time for themselves. Over 40% of teachers report feeling high stress every day during the school year, which ties teaching with nursing as having the highest stress rate of any career (Waterford, 2021.)

Causes of stress can include lack of resources, class behavioral problems, or pressure relating to standardized test expectations, to name a few. Still, they all lead to the same outcomes: weakened physical and emotional health (Waterford, 2021). When left unchecked, teacher stress can lead to burnout and contribute to a high teacher turnover rate in education. Therefore, self-care isn't just a good personal habit, but it's in your students' and colleagues' best interest, too. By eating well, sleeping enough, exercising, and finding other ways to take care of yourself, self-care can help you reach your potential in the classroom (and life), which will, in turn, help your students succeed, too (Wei, 2018).

Self-care is necessary for educators to maintain good mental health. When you take time for yourself, you can give the world your best. Follow the steps and rekindle your passion that propels your plan to action and purpose. Just choose one thing to do better today. Master it. Then, add another. I'm still on this journey too.

This is the most important principle but often the most neglected. Being STRONG is a mindset preparing your body, mind, and soul for success and students. Let's dive in and find out how to be STRONG to *be their warrior.*

13

S- STOP AND REMEMBER YOUR WHY

Passion propels purpose

*I*t all started when my oldest son, giddy with excitement, began first grade. As we were packing and preparing his backpack and clothes for his first day of first grade, he asked me if I'd walk him into his new class. I reminded him that since I'm a teacher, I couldn't miss my first day of school. (I worked in a different district.) I reassured him that his dad would take him. His bright eyes glazed over with tears, which pierced my heart as he said, "But I wanted *you* to be there for me."

"I'm sorry, buddy. I can't."

He firmly stated, "Then why did you become a teacher?" He challenged me that day. I defined my *why* that day for my son. I did it before "your *why*" was trendy and became a t-shirt logo. But knowing it got me through. It took everything in me to summon the desire to greet 22 eager first graders, and none of them was my own son. I needed to muster enthusiasm like 100 wiggling puppies welcoming you to greet my students for the first time. Even though my heart knew my son needed me, I knew others needed me also. I had the opportunity to influence more than one life. Little faces smiled back at me as I greeted them. Reluctant parents' nerves were soothed as I smiled at them, reassuring them that their child would have a great day. At the end of the day, my son and I celebrated his first day with his favorite ice cream. It all worked out because my *why* got me through. It still does. So I challenge you as my six-year-old challenged me: Why are you an educator?

Knowing your *why* will get you through difficult days. Some days I feel like I'm drowning in data and stifled by bureaucratic demands feeling defeated; they make me feel like I'm not making a difference. But then I remind myself of my *why*. My creativity climbs, and I refocus on what kids need. Knowing my *why* keeps me going. Otherwise, the system will slay me.

Some days I even chant part of my *why*: "I get to inspire and encourage children. I get to love them. I get to influence them and show them they matter. I get to make a difference." (For some, this may be silly, but I genuinely believe affirming words out loud set you up for success. Instead of drowning in demands, the kids and their needs become your focus.) Knowing my *why* helps me stay focused on kids. When doubt creeps in, passion pushes it out.

Keep in mind, your *why* may change. Therefore, revisit it frequently. For example, one year, my *why* was a photo of a student who was over-the-top needy. Your big idea, *why*, will probably remain the same, like making a difference, but your reason to keep going daily can change. Currently, my *why* expands to educators. I want to help new and seasoned teachers stay passionate for *all* kids. So, revisit your *why* often and dig below the surface level *why* to what will motivate you and keep you going day-to-day.

Steve Jobs, the co-founder of Apple Inc., said, *"Your work is going to fill a large part of your life, and the only way to be truly satisfied is to do what you believe is great work. And the only way to do great work is to love what you do."* Remember that when you love what you do, your passion propels your purpose, and you'll do great work. Knowing your *why* keeps your passion alive.

Therefore, you've got to know your *why*. Post it where you can see it. Say it out loud. Knowing your *why* will remind you of your passion and purpose, propelling you to keep going. When you feel deflated and defeated, your *why* allows you to be their warrior despite current circumstances. It's not always easy to remind yourself to stay focused on your *why*, but every child and colleague needs you and is counting on you. Start STRONG. Stop and remember your *why* and be their warrior.

NEXT STEPS:

1. What is your *why*?
2. Will you commit to writing it down and making it a priority?
3. How will you be intentional with centering your life around your *why* this week?

CONNECT:

Your *why* has the power to inspire and encourage others. Please share your *why* using the hashtag #BeTheirWarrior. Let's connect and share our stories.

14

T- TAKE TIME TO THANK

An attitude of gratitude leads to a healthy mind and body.

*I*f happiness were a pill, I think the whole world would pop it. Thankfully, you and I don't need a pill to be happy. Do you want to be happy? Truly happy? Be grateful. Studies show that grateful people are happier. In fact, people that sent a text, letter, or e-mail of thanks to somebody who helped them, stayed in a better mood for up to a month. Gratitude grants seven scientific psychological benefits: It opens the door to better relationships, improves physical health, enhances empathy, reduces aggression, improves sleep, improves self-esteem, reduces stress, and increases mental strength (Morin, 2015). Gratitude is a mindful awareness of the benefits of life. So sign me up for a lifetime subscription to gratitude (Lucado, 2019).

Recount the good things in your professional and private life. Let them swirl in your soul and shine through your smile. Whether you choose to write a few sentences in a gratitude journal or simply take a moment to acknowledge all that you have, giving thanks silently transforms your life.

Many days as an educator, I feel like nothing goes right. I'll never forget when a parent was allowed to visit my class to see if I would be a good fit for her rising first grader. I was a competent teacher who felt like I'd never stepped into a classroom. I had students crawling on the floor, hitting each other, yelling, and making farting and burping noises. You name it. They did it! They had an audience. My background knowledge of them from spending day in and day out with them allowed me to filter their behavior. It was their natural response to anxiety. Most of my students didn't deal well with transitions or unknown variables. Having a new face in our room was an unknown variable. Although I felt embarrassed and incompetent, I had to stop and take time to be thankful. I had to remember how far my students had come from the beginning of the year. I focused on the triumphs, not the current trials. It's not always easy to do, especially when you're under the microscope of a judging parent. Needless to say, her child didn't end up in my class. (I wonder why?)

Another time, my attention was drawn to redirecting a child who was disrupting, distracting, demanding attention, and destroying property. When he was displaying undesirable behavior, I wanted to roar like a lion. Instead, I mustered the gumption to speak softly and kindly. But truly, I was angry because, once again, he had stolen the learning time of 21 other deserving students. Can you relate? (If not, you already have something to add to your thankful list.) Resentment happens, but then I take time to thank; it reframes everything.

On tough days, I went home and drowned my difficult day in self-pity and wine. I told myself wine helped me not see the weeds in my life. It numbed overwhelming emotions. I told myself that I *needed* a glass of wine to cope with the stress of my day. Then one glass turned to two and three. It went from wine only on the weekend to my daily wine (whine) time. I started to feel sluggish and gained weight. My attitude waned. That's when it dawned on me there was a better way. I exchanged self-pity for gratitude. I pulled in the reins on wine. I didn't need it to cope with challenging days and challenging students. What I needed was to be STRONG in every way, taking care of myself and my attitude, filling up with gratitude. As educators, our days are challenging and emotionally charged. The struggle to cope is real, but we can rechannel our thoughts, emotions, and actions for positive results in our lives.

Sometimes the everyday challenges of what you do threatens to swallow you. Therefore it's imperative to take time to express gratitude. Thank you, thank you, thank you! Three is a good number. It is aesthetically pleasing in nature. Three wishes get granted. And the third time's a charm—magical marvelous three. I dare you to write down three things for which you are grateful every day. When you do, you will experience your mood lift upward toward the sun. You'll experience happiness, which leads to more and more gratitude. I graze throughout the day on gratitude. One thankful thought leads me to another and another. Taking time to thank focuses your mind on what is essential in your life, reminding you that all you do is worth it. Be thankful.

We don't get to pick and choose our kids or circumstances, but we get to choose our response to them. Choose to be grateful. Thanking reframes the scenario and our thinking, changing bleak to bright. Thanking releases serotonin in the brain and body, leaving you and me happy with lifted spirits. Happy thoughts produce happy actions. (The opposite is also true; negative thoughts produce negative outcomes.) Thanking fulfills.

5 SIMPLE STEPS TO TAKE TIME TO THANK

1. Daily Trio: Write down or stop and think of three things that you're thankful for.
2. Thank a colleague or family member
3. Create a thankful journal and write in it daily
4. Mindful moment: Think of one moment in your day that was good. If it was 99% bad, look for 1% good.
5. Alphabetize your blessings. For example, A: ability to inspire students, B: bees, butterflies, & blooms, C: cats, curious children, E: embracing family, etc.

Educators experience highs, lows, happy, sad, elated, and deflated days. When working with challenging children- all children- focus on the triumphs, not the trials. Remember the child that I shared about who I sometimes felt resentment towards because he, unknowingly, stole learning time from others? His growth in learning is a triumph that I cling to. The other day, he built a catapult with a partner. It worked. He experienced success. Witnessing him working with a partner was a success for me. His personal success was seeing an object whirl and hurl through the air, precisely landing in a bucket. Priceless emotion seeped out his pores.

When we made ice cream, his smile and the skip in his step dimmed disappointments and trials. The day we made ice cream, he proclaimed it to be the best day of school ever! (Just the day before, he yelled at me, stating that he hated school.) He went from displaying anger and growling at others as he passed by them to hugging me, saying, "I love you, Mrs. Hall." And in those moments, the magnitude of what we do washes over me. We have lives to mold. We make a difference. Our responsibility is great, but our rewards are greater. Give thanks in the hard times, too, because they lead to more joyous victories.

Every Monday morning, I have butterflies in my stomach because I'm overwhelmed and reminded of the awesome responsibility we have shaping tiny humans. It's hard and exhausting work inspiring, encouraging, meeting each and every unique need, and helping every single student succeed. But it's rewarding too. It's something I don't take lightly. So, for me, every morning is like the opening night of a theater production. (I'm just as excited and nervous to get it right too.) Before the curtains are drawn, and the first line is spoken, I must take time to thank.

"*When you have an Attitude of Gratitude, you wake up saying thank you.*" Maya Angelou knew the importance of taking the time to be thankful. It's good for your health and happiness.

NEXT STEPS:

1. If you don't have one already, start a gratitude journal.
2. Daily Thankful Trio- What are three things you are thankful for today?
3. Thank a colleague. Make a conscious effort to thank at least one colleague a day or week. Put it on your calendar or set a reminder on your phone.
4. Remember to focus on your triumphs not your trials. Write them down so you can revisit them.

CONNECT:

Connect with other warrior teachers and share what you do on Twitter or Instagram. **Share how you take time to be thankful. What were the results?** Your stories and pictures may be just what someone needs for encouragement to be a warrior for their students. You make a difference. Let's create a community, a movement that amplifies *all* students. Use the hashtag #BeTheirWarrior.

15

R- REST & REVIVE

Rejuvenate your body and mind through rest. Discover ways physical self-care revives you.

*R*est is renewing, rejuvenating, and reviving. Rest restores brain and body cells. Rest is a natural rhythm in nature and life. "Rest is fundamental to good health, both physically and mentally. People who are sleep deprived have less energy, difficulty focusing on tasks, and find it harder to maintain optimal physical fitness" (Guardian, 2017). Sufficient sleep boosts our memory and ability to learn new information. Rest is necessary and vital to renewal and performance.

Teachers get about six hours of sleep each night on average. Is this enough? It's recommended that adults need an average of eight hours. High-stress levels make it difficult to sleep, hence reducing the amount educators get (Guardian, 2017). Since teaching is a stressful job, you need to develop a bedtime habit that quiets your mind and body to prepare for sleep. When you do, you get a good night's rest, ready to face a new day.

I'm intentional about no electronic devices two hours before I plan to go to bed. When I don't do this, it leaves me sleepless tossing and turning between my sheets for hours. Ensuring proper sleep guarantees my productivity and positivity. Like you, I want to be my best for my students. Proper sleep optimizes my ability to be mentally and physically available to meet each and every need of my students. Ample sleep gives me the edge to arrive early and prepare my day; excellent provisioning and planning free me to pour into relationships.

Remember my story of total humiliation when I called my principal because I was tapped out, burned out? I reached a breaking point because I loved my students so much. I pushed myself too far, giving and giving. I worked every day, including weekends, to meet each and every need. What *gives* when you give so much? Your health and peace of mind. There is a better way. When we take care of ourselves, we are *truly* loving our students. Self-care gives you an edge while self-neglect causes crisis and cripples performance.

Slowing down can lead to great change. Joy and hurry are incompatible. Being effective weakens with weariness. I've learned to say *no* to some things creating space for a meaningful *yes*. Say *yes* to what inspires and refuels passion.

What fills your bucket? What refuels and restores you? The following is an example of my bucket list. (And I don't mean *kick the bucket* list. I totally mean what fills you up.)

MY SELF-CARE PLAN - FILL MY BUCKET LIST

1. Nature. Getting outside for a walk or sitting soaking up sun rays. Listening to a bubbling fountain.
2. Just sitting still watching birds, bees, and butterflies.
3. Time with my family and friends.
4. Reading
5. Journal writing
6. Exercise
7. Finishing one thing I've started
8. Meditation time
9. Weekly massage
10. Recreation- Balance is the key to stress. Are you regularly setting aside time for rest and recreation? The word "recreation" literally means to create again. It means to restore and refresh. When you are burned out, there is nothing left to give. Be sure to intentionally plan recreation. What do you do for fun?

 **Try This**

      Create your own "Fill My Bucket List." Use it to guide your proactive self-care plan. Incorporate self-care into your rhythms and routines as opposed to adding to a "to do" list. Self-care is a systematic habit instead of one more thing to do.

My instructional coach shared the following quote: "*Schedule your priorities instead of prioritizing your schedule.*" Make time for your priorities in life, instead of prioritizing a "to do" list. Because I love my learners, I schedule

> "**Self-care is a systematic habit instead of one more thing to do.**"

my priorities. I rest, refuel, and fill my bucket so that I can pour into theirs.

Slowing down offers time for reflection and growth. Slowing down and filling my bucket recharges me. When I go have a cup of cappuccino with a friend, I leave with a leap in my spirit and a skip in my step. I'm recharged and ready to roll. The following quote by Anne Lamott captures what happens after you pause and fill your bucket: "*Almost everything will work again if you unplug it for a few minutes, including you.*"

How will you slow down and recharge? One way is to protect your time. Build some white space into your schedule. Love yourself enough to set boundaries. Your time and energy are precious; you get to choose how you use them. John D. Rockefeller noted, "*Don't be afraid to give up the good to go for the great.*" Boundaries allow you to say no to *good* things, so you have time to say yes to *great* things.

One boundary I have is saying *yes* to things that have a definite starting and stopping point. If there's no starting and stopping date, count me out. I can do many things for a short time, but I wouldn't say I like doing things infinitely. I used to say *yes* to every opportunity. I had so many balls in the air. It was only a matter of time before I crashed. And I did. It wasn't a fun way to learn to instill boundaries. Therefore, know what you *will* and *won't* do ahead of time. Set your criteria for saying yes. Now, when opportunities come my way that don't match my criteria, it's easy to say no.

Remember, there are seasons for yes and seasons for no. When I had small children, I said no more often. I gave 100% while at school then left to be with my babies. Now that my babies are grown up, I say yes more often if it fits my criteria. I say yes when I can use my gifts and talents, and the activity fills me.

Setting boundaries with your time, allowing white space in your agenda, can be hard if you are a people pleaser. Often, people say *yes* for approval. When you know your *why* and what fills your bucket, you'll center your responses around your priorities instead of over-scheduling and trying to prioritize activities that drain and stress you out, but you do out of obligation. Focus on your passion, refuel, and set your boundaries.

Refuel with nutritious food. Simple right? (We know we're supposed to do this, but yet I stuff my face with gummy bears.) Can you imagine a champion swimmer or any professional athlete's performance if they neglected proper rest and refueling their bodies with strengthening food? Refuel with energy-giving food. A healthy body leads to productive performance.

What would happen if you put low-quality gas in a Mercedes Benz? It wouldn't perform optimally; It would spit and sputter and yield lower gas mileage. Mercedes Benz and other luxury cars have a label on their gas lid, informing consumers only to use premium gas. Premium leads to maximum gas mileage and smooth running. They perform better on premium, and so do we. Good nutritious food yields more mileage and higher performance. It's not about diet or weight. It's about healthy habits and filling our bodies with healthful foods that revive to go the extra mile for our students.

Being STRONG includes rest, recreation, and rejuvenation, which restores our soul. Restoration refuels our passion.

NEXT STEPS:

1. What is one thing you can do to scale back your schedule allowing for more rest?
2. What fills your bucket? Prioritize it today. Work to do just one thing a day that fills your bucket.
3. In what ways can you make healthier food choices to refuel your body with power?

CONNECT:

Connect with other warrior teachers and share what you do on Twitter or Instagram. **Share how you fill your bucket. What do you do to rest and revive? What were the results?** Your stories and pictures may be just what someone needs for encouragement to be a warrior for their students. You make a difference. Let's create a community, a movement amplifying *all* students. Use the hashtag #BeTheirWarrior.

16

O- OMIT NEGATIVE

Harnessing and replacing negative thoughts and habits with positive ones promotes a sound mind and actions.

$\mathcal{A}$ post on social media enlightened me. Although it isn't anything, we don't feel or face, seeing the post brought to light many educators' frustrations. The post posed the following question: "If you had a magic wand, what would you change?" The responses were resounding:

- Meetings- there are too many meetings and not enough prep time
- Mandates- too many initiatives to implement
- Focus- mandates change before they're mastered, often changing every two years
- Paperwork- there's too much paperwork
- Testing- there is too much testing

- Behavior management - lack of good systems and follow-through
- Class size- smaller class sizes lead to better relationships and higher student achievement
- Social, emotional lessons and emphasis are needed more than standardized tests

While these are educators' reality and truly burdensome, we can't change *everything*. (I wish we could. Where's my magical wand?) But we *can* focus on what we can do and change. We can't omit all these negative situations, but we *can* stay positive when it looks like everything is crumbling. We *can* look for solutions instead of staying stuck on problems. We *can* replace negative with positive.

A piece of the self-care puzzle is mental health, which begins in our minds. When we manage our thoughts, they manage our responses and emotions. Let's focus on what we *can* do and omit the negatives. In Maya Angelou's words, "*If you don't like something, change it. If you can't change it, change your attitude.*"

According to current research, more people feel anxious, hopeless, and fearful now more than ever. Yet, we have more advances in technology and more opportunities now than at any other time in history. Studies also indicate that to be happy, hope is essential. Hope sees opportunities in challenges. Hope is a positive outlook. Hope omits negative thoughts that something isn't going to work out. Personally, without hope, I couldn't get up and face another day. Hope invigorates me to give it one more shot. To give it my best. Hope says, "It's going to be better with your best efforts."

A bad day in education doesn't mean you're a bad teacher, it's a bad school, a bad class, or a bad career choice. For some reason, many of us ruminate, rehearse, revisit, and replay events that produce more worry and negative thoughts. A bad day happens to everyone. Deborah Day declared, "*Lighten up on yourself. No one is perfect. Gently accept your humanness.*"

Remember, tomorrow is a new day to start fresh and make a difference. We all have bad days, weeks, and sometimes seasons. Remember your *why*, rest and revive, omit negative thoughts and actions, and move on.

The beauty of morning is that it's a brand new day. We give our learners grace to start over each day. Let's be sure to extend the same to ourselves. Give yourself a fresh start each day.

When hard times and negative thoughts are invading your mind, pause. Refocus on rewards. The rewards in teaching are priceless and plentiful. I feel like a celebrity when I walk down the halls or into the cafeteria. I hear, "Hi, Mrs. Hall." I see arms waving and hands signing the "I love you" sign. Past students come and sneak a hug before they go to their class. I care, and they know it. When students overcome a struggle, I'm rewarded by their progress and perseverance. I love the smile of accomplishment on their faces. When students voluntarily show empathy and compassion for others, and when a student who has selective mutism shares their work in a loud, confident voice, I'm rewarded. Seeing students' learning transfer beyond a lesson, I'm rewarded. When a student that I had sixteen years ago, writes "You recognized the good in me. I have always felt so blessed to have you as my teacher. You helped shape me and my life," I'm rewarded. Cling to hope and find something positive in your challenges. You'll be rewarded.

WONDERFUL WAYS TO OMIT NEGATIVITY

- **Surround yourself with positive people and media.** Be intentional about who you hang out with and what you read and watch.

A story's told of a man who put an eagle's egg into a chicken nest. The eagle hatched and grew up with the brood of chickens. All his life, he did what the chickens did: scratching the dirt for seeds and insects, clucking, and never flying more than a few feet off the ground. One day he saw a magnificent bird soaring gracefully above the barnyard. He asked the chickens what it was called. They replied, "It's an eagle, king of all birds. But don't give him any mind because you could never be like him(Johnson, 2018).

Potential progresses or regresses based upon our relationships. I've often heard: we become like the last five books we've read and the five people we spend time with. What goes in our minds comes out, and who we hang out with rubs off. We get to choose.

- **Practice thought management. Pick what you ponder.** The following story perfectly illustrates managing your attitude and thoughts.

Worried that their son was too optimistic, the parents of a little boy took him to a psychiatrist. In an attempt to dampen the boy's spirits, the psychiatrist showed him into a room piled high with nothing but horse manure. Instead of displaying distaste, the little boy clambered to the top of the pile and began digging.

"What are you doing?" the psychiatrist asked.

"With all this manure," the little boy replied, beaming, "there must be a pony in here somewhere" (Mintz, 2012).

You can choose to focus on the crap or the prize.

- **Focus.** I like what Steve Jobs says, "*One of my mantras— focus and simplicity. Simple can be harder than complex; you have to work hard to get your thinking clean to make it simple. But it's worth it in the end because once you get there, you can move mountains.*"
- **Flush negative—replace with positive.** You can't focus on two thoughts at the same time, so replace negative thoughts with positive thoughts.

- **Think happy thoughts.** Happiness and well-being are important. They help protect against mental and physical disorders. (Please note that there are true medical, mental disorders that require more attention than omitting negative thoughts. I'm not naive about those. In fact, I'm filled with empathy as I've walked through darkness with students and friends. However, positive thoughts will bring more light than negative thoughts.)

- **Take time to celebrate.** Celebration is a pivotal stage in the productivity and positivity process because it allows us to commemorate all the good that we do. Celebrating helps us stay in the present moment. Celebrating reminds me of how far I've come instead of how inadequate I may think I am or feel. Especially because I tend to focus on all I still want to accomplish. "Celebration feeds our basic human need for self-love and self-acceptance. Celebration is emotional nourishment" (Volkar,2008). Celebrating creates an environment for more wins. Like I've stated previously in this book: Success breeds success. When you celebrate, you focus on wins instead of losses. Positive instead of negative.

- **Celebrate daily, weekly, and monthly.** Celebration is self-acknowledgement and recognition for successfully completing every small step you take forward in your life. I break down my personal victories into three parts: *Daily Delights, Weekly Wins,* and *Monthly Milestones.* Each day, usually on my drive home from work or when I brush my teeth before bed, I reflect on happy moments from the day.

Sometimes, I write them down in my planner so I can revisit the celebration for the day. Every Friday, I write down my personal "wins" for the week. They can be as simple as staying hydrated or thanking a colleague. Then, at the end of each month, I write down all the positive things that I did or happened for the month. By doing this, I take my eyes off my challenges and focus on gratitude and positivity. "Celebration is positive magnification. What we focus on expands" (Volkar, 2008).

- **Remember to be kind to yourself.** The master of laughter, Lucille Ball, reminds *"Love yourself first, and everything else falls in line. You really have to love yourself to get anything done in this world."*

Filter your thoughts and people in your life. Omit negative and negative triggers to stay strong and conquer challenges. Focus only on what you can change. Start with that. You can do it. Be STRONG and omit negative to be their warrior.

NEXT STEPS:

1. What is one negative thought you can replace with a positive thought?
2. How can you remove negative triggers in your life? (Just start with one.)
3. In what ways can you connect with positive people?

CONNECT:

Connect with other warrior teachers and share what you do on Twitter or Instagram. **Share how you omitted negative** thoughts/people and replaced them with positive ones. **What were the results?** Your stories and pictures may be just what someone needs for encouragement to be a warrior for their students. You make a difference. Let's create a community, a movement amplifying *all* students. #BeTheirWarrior

N- NEVER GIVE UP

You and your learners are worth whatever it takes to keep striving toward goals.

*R*emember the rebound and mistakes are for learning concepts from chapter 5? Rebound is the advice my friend, Helen Stanphil, shared with one of my writing classes and me. Well, there is more to the story. Helen crafted a story where the main character, Penelope Pepper, was struggling with playing basketball. Penelope wasn't making any baskets, and she couldn't run fast and dribble the ball at the same time. During practice one day, her coach arranged everyone in a semi-circle around the basketball hoop, announcing that they would work on rebounds. He informed them that in basketball, if you shoot and miss, a rebound is a second chance. It's wonderful; you get a second chance with every shot you take. Like basketball, if you and I keep shooting, eventually, something will go in. Stick. Make a difference. Like in basketball, the next swish—success—is just around the bend or in the rebound. In what areas are you struggling? Seize opportunities. Rebound.

Often, we give up when the miracle was just one meeting, one step, one lesson, or one hug away. Keep going. Pursue your dreams. Go after the needs of *all* students. When you feel you've exhausted every avenue and feel knocked down, get up and try one more time. Never give up on kids or yourself. After all, when you rebound and keep doing your best, you'll be a winner even if the scoreboard doesn't show it.

An unexpected tear slid down my cheek as the reality of this vulnerable statement from a Twitter tweet penetrated my heart: "After 12 years in, I'm tired. Teaching is hard, but sometimes maybe you just need a change. I wanna take risks. I wanna be better." I wonder how many of us feel this way? We've got to go from burned out to burning with passion. But how?

Be STRONG. Connect with others who inspire you to keep going. Stop and remember your *why*. Take time to thank. Rest and revive. Omit negative thoughts, and never give up. Seek help.

Why is it so hard to seek help? I think we feel inadequate as an educator when we can't solve problems ourselves. We need others. It's okay to need help.

When I feel like exiting education, I know it's time for a change. So if you are on the edge of exiting, try making a change in education before giving up on it.

 Try This

- Change grade levels. Maybe a different grade would be a better fit.
- Change education roles. For example, I left a general education class to be a STEM teacher. Switching roles gives me new challenges to conquer and keeps my passion alive. It can for you too.
- Find mentors who you trust to work with you through your options and emotions.
- Remember to fill yourself and be STRONG.

Each day I work to combat negative thoughts and situations in my mind and life. I can't camp out there. If I did, I wouldn't have the stamina to keep going and doing what is best for kids. Each day I begin again fresh and new to bring the best to students. I give myself a break by forgetting yesterday's mistakes. (It's what we do for our students, right? We give them a fresh start, a redo each day. Why should we do anything less for ourselves?) It's an ongoing process. Remember "progress, not perfection." Perfection stops me dead in my tracks every time and reminds me that if I don't measure up, I might as well give up. Giving up on reaching *all* kids and doing what is best isn't an option; therefore, I keep going one step at a time toward a goal for them and toward a goal for me. Keep going. We're given a choice...an opportunity to make a *big* difference or stay stuck and give up. What if we rock the world with hope? What if we pursue priorities and passions like there's no tomorrow?

We have an obligation to keep uplifting and encouraging each other and taking risks. People depend on us. Never let challenges define you and stop you. Honestly, I've almost given up on writing this book more times than I can count. It's stretched me, it's made me think, and it's made me discipline my time. What kept me going were a couple of trusted friends and colleagues who provided kind, specific, and helpful feedback. Above all, they encouraged and told me that I could when I thought I couldn't. They reminded me to stay focused on my *why*. You see, I deeply want to inspire educators like you and help them feel passionate, energized, and filled with strategies, so they lead all learners to their full potential. When you are energized and have strategies that work for your students, you'll have more time and fulfillment in your life. So the cycle will repeat. Therefore, I continued to write. Find your trusted few friends and colleagues and cling tightly to them.

6 TIPS TO HELP YOU KEEP GOING TOWARD YOUR PASSION & PURPOSE

1. Start with a positive mindset.
2. Exhaust every intervention, modification, and resource to help a child. Never give up on them.
3. Exhaust every resource to help yourself. Seek a counselor, a coach, a class, or whatever it takes. Never give up on yourself.
4. Don't "should on" yourself. Focus on where you need to go, not what you should have done.
5. Recognize your gifts and goals. Exhibit determination and discipline toward those goals using your gifts.
6. Remember the wise words of Babe Ruth: "*It's hard to beat someone who never gives up.*"

To keep going, dedicate yourself to a process. It's a journey to reach goals, not a microwave meal. According to psychologist Jeremy Dean, research suggests that taking 21 days to form a habit is probably right, as long as all you want to do is drink a glass of water after breakfast. Anything *harder* is likely to take longer to become a solid habit, and, in the case of some activities, much longer (Popova, 2016).] Give yourself some grace and space to take time to reach what you're striving for. It will take time, but it'll be worth it.

Quit limiting yourself and be good to yourself. I just love the following story because it illustrates how we can easily give up. It's a great analogy for how we create paradigms in our lives and end up limiting our potential. The story goes something like this...

> *When fleas are placed in a jar, they try to jump out – but after the lid is placed on, the fleas stop attempting the escape – as they learn the boundaries of the new environment*

they're in. Even when the lid is removed, the fleas never jump out. Their thinking has created the 'lid' as the boundary, so it has conditioned them to limit their jumping. We're all a bit like those fleas – our thinking conditions us. It creates imaginary boundaries and limited ways of thinking that keep us stuck in a certain way of operating. Our thinking creates our view of reality, and we don't even realize we're doing it. (Palethorpe, 2017).

Maybe in the past, you've had ideas that were truly best for kids, but you were told you couldn't do it by the administration or colleagues. Well, maybe now you have a new administration. Try again. Always try again when it comes to doing what is best for kids or going after a goal that is on fire in your gut. Don't put an imaginary lid on your life, your dreams, and your ideas. Keep jumping.

In the words of Steve Jobs, "*The people who are crazy enough to think they can change the world are the ones who do.*" Start STRONG and never give up. Remember to rebound. Rebounds win the game.

NEXT STEPS:

1. What is one step you can take toward your goal today?
2. Remember to rebound. If you get off track, what step can you take today to keep going in the direction of your dreams and goals for your students? For you?
3. In what ways can you connect with positive people in your life that keep you going?

CONNECT:

Connect with other warrior teachers and share what you do on Twitter or Instagram. **Share how you keep going and never give up** on a student or yourself when you feel like giving up. What were the results? Your stories and pictures may be just what someone needs for encouragement to be a warrior for their students. You make a difference. Let's create a community, a movement amplifying *all* students. Use the hashtag #BeTheirWarrior

G- GO DEEPER

Continue to grow personally and professionally, igniting passion for doing what's best for *all* students.

I heard a sigh as my colleague waded through her email messages. "What is it?" I inquired. Exasperated, she responded with a resounding, "Our professional development day will be spent in meetings *all* day. We have no time to work in our rooms." Have you ever felt like this? I don't think educators dislike professional development. I think what they don't like is having their time dictated and monopolized with monotonous meetings. Educators love to learn. Like your students, I think you like to learn about what you are interested in. What if your professional development was more personal? What if you got to select your learning? Wouldn't it be great to design your professional development instead of designed by others who think they know what is best for your kids?

Let's create a movement. Let's start asking the same questions to our leadership and their leadership. Our students crave and need voice and choice accompanied by relevant learning opportunities, and so do we.

Research shows that educators who invest in themselves and participate in ongoing professional development stick around for the long haul and are fueled with more passion. In fact, an inspiring and informed teacher is the most important school-related factor influencing student achievement. Great teachers help create great students. So it is critical to pay close attention to how we train and support both new and experienced educators(Edutopia, 2008).

Ongoing professional development keeps teachers up-to-date on new research on how children learn, emerging technology tools for the classroom, new curriculum resources, and more. The best professional development is ongoing, experiential, collaborative, and connected to and derived from working with students and understanding their culture(Edutopia, 2008). Going deeper isn't just for students. Educators need deeper learning too.

Gather knowledge and information for transformation. Many proclaim knowledge is power and the key to learning. I'm afraid I have to disagree. Knowing information isn't enough. Executing knowledge is key. Action leads to transformation in our students and us. When we truly transform our teaching, our kids grow. Too often, I've gone to a wonderful conference and received a SWAG bag filled with all the teaching things and goodies. I'd come home, fired up, and ready to conquer the world. Then...Monday morning came. The ideas were shelved. The SWAG bag was totally forgotten until summertime when I had time to implement my annual declutter cleaning frenzy, and I found it. Can you relate? So how do we keep going, growing, generating, and executing new ideas?

8 WAYS TO GO DEEPER

1. Be intentional. When you attend a conference, commit to implementing one new idea immediately. Once it becomes a habit, implement another. Write out a plan. I do this, so ideas don't get shelved. I take a risk to try something new while my excitement and enthusiasm are high.

2. Establish a network of like-minded people who continue to remind you of the best practices you just learned, who continue to stretch you, encourage you, and applaud your growth no matter how minuscule it may be. They see you blooming. They water the growth, so you continue to be STRONG. Your network can be in your own building, district, or all around the world.

Not so long ago, I learned about Professional Learning Networks (PLN) on Twitter. I've loved knowing that there is a whole wide world of knowledge, tips, encouragement, and connections from educators in the trenches that are just like me—wanting to make learning more relevant for our students and make a difference for *all* kids. I've learned different points of view and ideas to help students. And I get to do it in the comfort of my own home. Many of you will get what I'm talking about, but if you were like me and didn't get it, please jump onto the Twitter PLN party train. You'll build relationships, make connections, learn ideas that you can implement right away, and you'll grow as a professional and person.

3. Schedule it. I add Twitter chats to my calendar. I schedule webinars and podcasts. Determine how many you can manage a week or month and commit to scheduling it. When your growth is a priority, you'll schedule it.

4. Read. Set a goal to read a certain amount of pages a day or a certain amount of books a month. Read what you enjoy. You don't have to always read education books. Just read. You'll grow. (And according to research, relax.)

5. Step out of your comfort zone to go deeper. "You're so extra!" A colleague remarked. I don't do it to be recognized by others. I do it for students, for improved outcomes, and to create a love for learning. It's called passion, right? Go the extra mile to do whatever is necessary for your students, even if it's outside your wheelhouse and comfort zone.

For example, I'm not great at many of the new technology options for students. However, I saw an idea on Twitter that I knew my students would love. The idea I saw was using the ChatterPix App for kids. Students were able to make their own pictures talk by using the app. Shakey in my own ability, I enlisted the expertise of my instructional coach. She provided strong support, enabling me to step outside of my comfort zone. First grade students used the app to present their research project on an animal. They selected a picture of their animal, and the animal shared from its point of view information about its habitat, life cycle, etc. It was wonderful to see the students engaged in creating a narrative for their animal to share. It was super cute to see the students then share their "talking animals" with each other. My instructional coach helped me learn a new idea, which boosted students' success and engagement. Find your support and take a leap. It just might be the best thing ever.

6. Just do one thing more today than you did yesterday to grow and be better.

7. Grow personally by giving attention to your goals from chapter **15.** Be intentional about scheduling time to do what fills your bucket.

8. Try new things. A friend invited me to paint. Digging my heels into the ground, I refused. You see, I can't draw anything that resembles the picture in my mind. I never progressed past stick figures. My artistic abilities are null. So much so that when I was in high school, I skated past art class to the woodshop. I figured that since my dad had the same tools, I might have a fighting chance in *that* class. I didn't want the art class to mess up my Grade Point Average. Did I mention I'm terrible at art? After much coaxing and touting how much fun we'd have together, reluctantly, I wound up in a painting class with lots of ladies and loads of laughter. I went for fun, not a masterpiece. I didn't imagine I could ever paint anything that wouldn't wind up in the trash. I'm not an artist. (That's what I told myself, so it must be true.) You know what? Because of the teacher's passion and step-by-step directions, I ended up with something that resembled a painting. Even my youngest son said, "Wow, mom, you can hang that up on the wall." Now, I incorporate painting and drawing in class for my students more often. When we try new things, we have new things to try with our students. (Also, we get to remember what it feels like to try something new. It keeps us relatable for our learners.)

Growth can be scary sometimes. I know because I call myself a recovering perfectionist. I love learning; I'm a life-long learner but let's be real. I'm afraid to try new things if I can't get them to be picture perfect like in my mind. For example, years ago, my husband thought it would be a great idea for our whole family to build our own home. Mind you. We didn't have a contractor. We were the contractors, and we didn't have any prior experience. All I knew about houses was how to live in them and clean them, not construct them from the ground up. Needless to say, it was a strenuous journey that not only flexed our physical muscles but our relationship muscles.

On the brink of quitting on us and the house, I overcame mountainous obstacles. I'll never forget having to learn everything, including waterproofing and caulking all the windows in our house. I'd never caulked a window in my life. I knew how it was supposed to look, but when I did it, the white goop globbed or ran down the side of the house. I was completely frustrated because my skills didn't match the perfectly caulked window picture in my mind. Well, the job got done. Not to perfection but completed after much personal growth and self-talk pushing myself across the perfection barrier. I learned I *could* do hard things. So can you!

If you're plagued by perfection, allow yourself grace and space to make mistakes. The more you do, the more you let go of perfectionism. I wouldn't have written this book without encouragement from my husband. He encouraged me to write down my ideas. Then, a friend challenged me to contact publishers. On my own, I'm not that gregarious. I fear that what I do isn't good enough, or I'll make mistakes. The truth is that I don't play video games with my kids because I'm not good at them. I always see Mario from the game Mario Cart flying off the track into outer space. I only like to do what I'm good at doing. (I know, I know... fixed mindset.) I get paralyzed when the images and ideas in my mind don't match my abilities. It's ridiculous! I know. That's why it is important to stay STRONG and surround yourself with like-minded people who inspire and encourage you. With every baby step forward, confidence grows as well as your skills. Now, I don't have to know every detail or see the finish line to start. I'm a recovering perfectionist who knows I've got to try and take risks, or I'll never be anyone's warrior.

After almost three decades in education, I'm still growing. I love the process of instructional coaching and coaching rounds. Just when you think you may have everything mastered, the process teaches you something new. This happened to me. My instructional coach suggested I use Swivl to record my lessons. Swivl is a device that moves as you move around video recording. I recorded a lesson. My findings and reflections were as follows:

- I'm *way* more animated than I thought.
- It was validating. I've learned great strategies and best practices along the way that I apply.
- The students were totally engaged.
- The students' conversations were on target. They were on task and constructive with their conversations and feedback. (I loved hearing their conversations. When roaming the room in real-time and working with one group of students, the rich dialogue is missed with another. A Swivl video allows you to see and hear it all.)
- Their behavior was good because of the video. I told them I was videotaping so that I could see how to improve what I do and so I could see what they were doing. (I just might need to Swivl every class every day.)
- I followed the instructional framework. I even stated the learning objective.
- There is no downtime in my class.
- Real-time seems to be much faster in my brain than the reality on the video. I guess because I am thinking 20 steps ahead. Actually, the pacing is pretty good. (I usually feel too rushed.)
- I gave positive praise for expectations.
- It was a wonderful opportunity to fine-tune my skills.
- I had unreasonable expectations for clean up time for some students. They took longer to clean up than I thought was necessary. I thought they were off task. The video revealed that they were truly cleaning up and trying to do it well. So after viewing the video and seeing the whole picture, I went to those students and apologized and

praised them for trying their best to do what was expected in the time allotted.

I encourage you to video yourself for your own viewing and reflection. You are more of an edu-rockstar than you think, and you'll see where you can improve and grow. (Even if it's apologizing to students.)

"*Good leadership requires you to surround yourself with people of diverse perspectives who can disagree with you without fear of retaliation,*" Doris Kearns Goodwin, American biographer, historian, former sports journalist, and political commentator, wisely stated. Therefore, the Personal Development Framework is a recipe to sort through emotions and disagreements, leading to learning, growing, and cementing relationships without fear.

The following framework corresponds with deeper thinking and actions in your workplace and life. It allows you to reflect and grow in relationships.

PERSONAL DEVELOPMENT FRAMEWORK

1. What am I feeling?
2. Are those feelings valid?
3. Under the circumstances, did the people I was working with do the best they could?
4. Under the circumstances, did I do the best I could?
5. Are the people I'm working with going to act/respond this way whether I like it or not?
6. What can I learn from this?
7. How can I serve this person?

Peter Drucker, a famous management trainer, wrote, "*We now accept the fact that learning is a lifelong process of keeping abreast of change.*" That's so true. The best teachers are the ones who are constantly pushing themselves to learn about new research in their field. Whether teachers attend conferences or workshops, learn independently, or join collaborative learning communities, ongoing professional development is the key to quality education. It's important to ensure teachers can take advantage of the latest research in their classroom, know how to take risks by including new concepts, teaching approaches, and technology in the curriculum, and inspire each other (Nixon, n.d.).

In the words of Maya Angelou, "*Do the best you can until you know better. Then when you know better, do better.*" P.D. is personal and professional development. Have the courage to follow your heart and intuition and become all you were meant to be for yourself and your learners. Go deeper and grow.

NEXT STEPS:

1. What do you do to grow personally?
2. What do you do to grow professionally?
3. How will you invest in yourself tomorrow?

CONNECT:

Connect with other warrior teachers and share what you do on Twitter or Instagram. **Share how you go deeper to grow personally and professionally. What were the results?** Your stories and pictures may be just what someone needs for encouragement to be a warrior for their students. You make a difference. Let's create a community, a movement amplifying *all* students. Use the hashtag #BeTheirWarrior.

IN CLOSING

> *"We don't have to be extraordinary in any way. I can do what you can't do, you can do what I can't do, and together we can do great things."*
>
> — MOTHER TERESA

*Y*ou can be a warrior for *all* kids by creating a positive, caring culture that keeps kids coming back, building life-changing relationships, cultivating a community that meets every student's needs, and being STRONG.

We may sometimes feel we can't do much as individuals, but humanity is made up of individuals. As individuals, we influence our students and their families, our colleagues, and our own families. They influence our communities, and our communities influence nations.

I know educators lie awake at night trying to figure out how to help everyone, but sometimes, it isn't within our grasp. You may not be able to help everybody, but you can help somebody. Each one of us can reach one and make a difference. You have gifts and talents the world needs. Together, we do great things.

Implementing the strategies I've shared from the three principles: Culture, Community, and Being STRONG were game changers for my students and me. I hope they are for you too.

Remember, preparing your mind and body by starting STRONG helps prevent burnout and ignites passion and purpose.

Be STRONG

S- Stop and Remember Your WHY

T- Take Time To Thank

R- Rest & Revive

O- Omit Negative

N- Never Give Up

G- Go Deeper

Plan to do something more today than you did yesterday to take better care of yourself and reach *all* kids. You may not influence millions, but you may influence the *one* who influences millions.

I implore you to be a warrior for *all* kids. Let the following statement punctuate your day, your life: *You* make a difference!

ACKNOWLEDGMENTS

Writing a book seems easy, right? It's a magnanimous project. I couldn't have pulled it off alone. I'm forever grateful for vision casters, graphic guides, advisors, editors, polishers, leaders, readers, and cheerleaders. Thank you for sharing your gifts and talents with me to share this message with the world. You've made this possible.

Everyone should have a knight in shining armor. Mine is David, my husband. He's gallant, selflessly serving our family and supporting my every endeavor. Thank you, David, my anchor, and best friend.

Brent, Collin, and all my school kids, thank you for giving me purpose. I love you and believe in you.

I'm so thankful for Rolodex people. You deserve a medal for helping me wrangle and organize my wandering thoughts.

Haley Cooprider, thank you for organizing me. (It all started with an ebook.) Thank you for being a fabulous "think" partner. Thank you for reading and tweaking and reading and tweaking the early stages. You're an admirable asset to anyone's life.

Kristy Buggs, thank you for calling me a champion for kids. Thank you for reading the proposal and providing kind, helpful, and specific feedback. You are classy and an admirable leader. Thank you for being a warrior for *all* kids and reflecting sunshine everywhere you go.

Natalie Street, I'm in awe of you. Your coaching abilities are exemplary. Your love and care for others radiate through your smile. Thank you for always cheering me on, supporting me, and reading the proposal. Like all you do, your feedback was helpful and insightful.

Michelle Pealo, I hit the lottery when my room assignment was next to you. Thank you for taking my ideas and making them a reality. The warrior title graphic is perfect thanks to you. Thank you for a listening ear, tech tips, and truly being concerned for others. You're a gem.

Jacie Maslyk meeting you at VCEC (Virginia Children's Engineering Conference) was a divine appointment. There are no words for how kind you were to read my proposal and give kind, specific, and helpful feedback. I'm a better writer and person because I know you.

Sarah Thomas and the whole EduMatch team. Wow! I'm in awe of you. Thank you for believing in me. I'm thrilled to be associated with kind, loving people who want what's best for *all* kids and educators. Thank you for working with me and providing an amazing family of educators. We're better together.

Refinement. I'm forever grateful for my focus group. Thank you for sanding off the rough edges of my manuscript. Thank you for believing in this project and being passionate about education. Your time is treasured.

Warriors: Dr. Markewitz and Rose Brandt.

Angie Miller, thank you for being a faithful friend and cheerleader. This project would have never come to fruition without your New Year's Day challenge. I'm so blessed to have someone who cares enough about me to keep pushing me out of my comfort zone, and that friend is you. Thank you for listening, reading, and laboring through this project with me. Thank you for your fun and adventures. You're the definition of a true friend.

Donna Hollowell, you're the best in every way. You are a treasured friend God dropped in my lap. I'm forever grateful. Thank you for your endless encouragement and attention to detail as you edited my rambling. (Not an easy task.) Thank you for being a loving, caring, and faithful friend. You're a gift.

REFERENCES

ASCD (2021, April 13). *7 Reasons why differentiated instruction works*. ASCD Inservice. https://inservice.ascd.org/7-reasons-why-differentiated-instruction-works/.

Acuff, J. (2018). *Finish: Give yourself the gift of done*. Portfolio/Penguin.

Alber, R. (2017, March 16). *Updating an age-old class activity*. Edutopia. https://www.edutopia.org/blog/updating-age-old-class-activity-rebecca-alber.

Alrubail, R. (2016, January 14). *Being mindful of cultural differences*. Edutopia. https://www.edutopia.org/discussion/being-mindful-cultural-differences.

Batterson, M. (2020). *Whisper: How to hear the voice of God*. Multnomah.

Berger, T. (2018, February 5). *An inside look at trauma-Informed practices*. Edutopia. https://www.edutopia.org/article/inside-look-trauma-informed-practices.

Burg, B., & Mann, J. D. (2015). *The go-giver: A little story about a powerful business idea*. Portfolio/Penguin.

Educate2Empower Publishing. (n.d.). https://e2epublishing. info/free-resources?rq=12%2Bencouraging%2Bphrases% 2Bto%2Bbuild%2Bresil.

Edutopia. (2008, March 17). *Why is teacher development important?: Because students deserve the best*. Edutopia. https://www.edutopia.org/teacher-development-introduction.

Goldberg, G., & Houser, R. (2017, July 19). *Battling decision fatigue*. Edutopia. https://www.edutopia.org/blog/battling-decision-fatigue-gravity-goldberg-renee-houser.

Guardian News and Media. (2017, September 12). *Why teachers should make sleep a priority*. The Guardian. https://www. theguardian.com/teacher-network/2017/sep/12/why-teachers-should-make-sleep-a-priority.

Harvard Health. (2011, July 01). *Music and health*. Harvard Health Publications. https://www.health.harvard.edu/staying-healthy/music-and-health

Jagodowski, S. (n.d.). *7 Fun ideas for morning meeting greetings for your class.* ThoughtCo. https://www.thoughtco.com/morning-meeting-greetings-ideas-4155217.

Johnson, R. (2018, April 12). *Destined to be an eagle.* Lighthouse of Hope Ministries. http://lighthouse-of-hope.org/fulfilling-our-purpose/destined-to-be-eagles.

King, H., & King, W. (2018). *The wild card: 7 steps to an educator's creative breakthrough.* Dave Burgess Consulting, Inc.

Kline, T. (n.d.). *Applying Maslow's hierarchy of needs In our classrooms.* ChangeKidsLives. http://www.changekidslives.org/actions-4.

Lewis, J. G. (2015, January 12). *Smells ring bells: How smell triggers memories and emotions.* Psychology Today. https://www.psychologytoday.com/us/blog/brain-babble/201501/smells-ring-bells-how-smell-triggers-memories-and-emotions.

Lucado, M. (2019). In *anxious for nothing: Finding calm in a chaotic world* (pp. 94–94). Thomas Nelson.

Minero, E. (2017, October 4). *When students are traumatized, teachers are too.* Edutopia. https://www.edutopia.org/article/when-students-are-traumatized-teachers-are-too.

Mintz, J. (2012, December 4). *There's got to be a pony somewhere.* Everywhere I Go. https://judymintz.com/2012/12/04/theres-got-to-be-a-pony-somewhere/.

Morin, A. (2015, April). *7 Scientifically proven benefits of gratitude.* Psychology Today. https://www.psychologytoday.com/us/blog/what-mentally-strong-people-dont-do/201504/7-scientifically-proven-benefits-gratitude.

Nixon, B. (n.d.). *4 Reasons teacher development matters.* Whitby School.

Palethorpe, M. (2017, November 23). *Are you a flea in jar?* Waypoint Partners. https://waypointpartners.co.uk/flea-in-jar/.

Pandolpho, B. (2018, January 24). *The power of sharing your story with students.* Edutopia. https://www.edutopia.org/article/power-sharing-your-story-students.

Paruthi, S., & Brooks, L. J. (2016, June 15). *Recommended amount of sleep for pediatric populations: A consensus statement of the American Academy of Sleep Medicine.* https://jcsm.aasm.org/doi/10.5664/jcsm.5866.

Person. (2008, July 15). *Why is assessment important?* Edutopia. https://www.edutopia.org/assessment-guide-importance.

Popova, M. (2016, July 8). *How long it takes to form a new habit.* Brain Pickings. https://www.brainpickings.org/2014/01/02/how-long-it-takes-to-form-a-new-habit/.

Powell, W., & Kusuma-Powell, O. (2011). *How to teach now: Five keys to personalized learning in the global classroom* (Chapter 1). ASCD.

Sussex Publishers. (n.d.). *Dopamine.* Psychology Today. https://www.psychologytoday.com/us/basics/dopamine.

Teach Me To Learn. (2014, April 30). *Research spotlight on parental involvement in education.* Teach Me To Learn at Home®. http://teachmetolearnathome.org/research-spotlight-on-parental-involvement-in-education/

Terada, Y. (2018, September 11). *Welcoming students with a smile.* Edutopia. https://www.edutopia.org/article/welcoming-students-smile.

Volker, T. (2008, April 22). Five good reasons to celebrate more often. https://coreu.com/five-good-reasons-to-celebrate-more-often/.

Walker, T. (n.d.). *The evidence is in: 'Happy' schools boost student achievement.* NEA. https://www.nea.org/advocating-for-change/new-from-nea/evidence-happy-schools-boost-student-achievement.

Watson, A. (2018, October 17). *The 2x10 strategy: a miraculous solution for behavior issues?* The Cornerstone For Teachers. https://thecornerstoneforteachers.com/the-2x10-strategy-a-miraculous-solution-for-behavior-issues/.

Waterford. (2021, May 17). *Why teacher self-care matters and how to practice self-care in your school.* Waterford.org. https://www.waterford.org/education/teacher-self-care *miraculous solution for behavior issues?*

Web DeskMaking Digital Information Accessible To The World. (2018, September 10). *The human attention span [INFOGRAPHIC].* Digital Information World. https://www.digitalinformationworld.com/2018/09/the-human-attention-span-infographic.html.

Wei, M. (2018, October 17). *Self-care for the caregiver.* Harvard Health. https://www.health.harvard.edu/blog/self-care-for-the-caregiver-2018101715003

ABOUT THE AUTHOR

(Photo: Emma Wynne Photography:
www.emmawynnephotography.com)

Pamela Hall, a multi national award-winning educator, is a speaker and author dedicated to helping educators consciously connect with and grow *all* learners. Pamela's a life-long learner leading and inspiring thousands of students and educators.

Pamela has appeared on PBS. and local news, and written for many magazines such as *Educator Insights*. She's a passionate educator who specializes in student relationships, class culture, engaging challenging students, and hands-on, life applicable learning. She encourages educators to be STRONG and embrace self-care.

Pamela leads *Literate For Life*, a non-profit foundation, that educates, encourages, and empowers children to be literate. She also shares tips on her mindfulness blog, a blog focused on amplifying all kids, education, and self-care. She's an ordinary cappuccino drinking, chocolate eating mom, and wife from Virginia with an extraordinary passion to make a positive difference.

Twitter: https://twitter.com/PamHall2inspire

Instagram: https://www.instagram.com/pamhall2inspire/

E-mail: pamhall2inspire@gmail.com

Website: https://www.pamhall2inspire.com

9 781953 852564